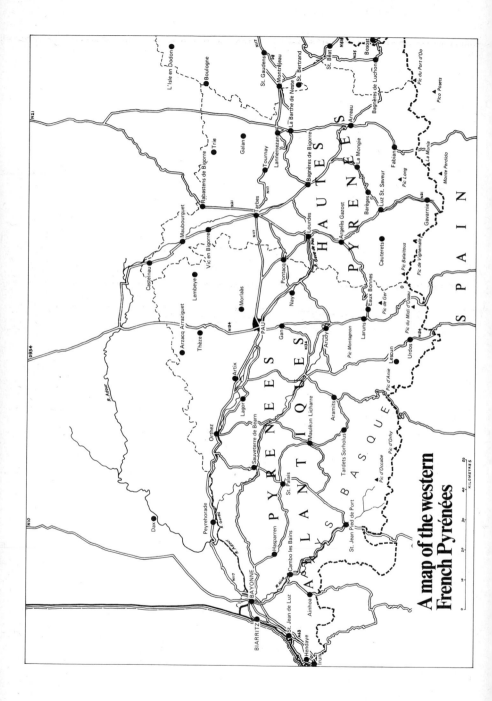

# A map of the western French Pyrénées

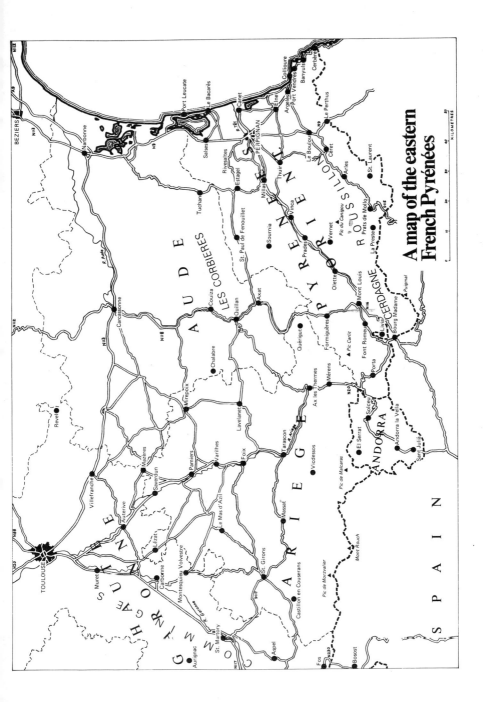

# A map of the eastern French Pyrénées

# History, People and Places in
# The French Pyrénées

# History, People and Places in
# The French Pyrénées

Neil Lands

SPURBOOKS LIMITED

Published by Spurbooks Limited
6 Parade Court, Bourne End,
Buckinghamshire.

ISBN 0 904978 92 3

British Library Cataloguing in Publication Data

Lands, Neil
    History, people and places in the French Pyrénées.
    1. Pyrénées — Description and travel
    I. Title
    914.4'89'0483            DC611.P988

    ISBN 0-904978-92-3

THIS BOOK IS FOR LEONARD AND JANET GORE

Designed and produced by
Mechanick Exercises, London

Printed in Great Britain by
McCorquodale (Newton) Ltd
Newton-le-Willows, Lancashire

# Contents

|     | Acknowledgements | 11 |
|-----|------------------|-----|
|     | List of Illustrations | 13 |
| 1   | An Historical Introduction | 15 |
| 2   | The Pays Basque | 27 |
| 3   | Béarn | 52 |
| 4   | Bigorre | 70 |
| 5   | Comminges and the Couserans | 87 |
| 6   | Ariège | 99 |
| 7   | Andorra and the Cerdagne | 111 |
| 8   | Roussillon | 125 |
| 9   | The Corbières | 141 |
| 10  | Information | 151 |
|     | Bibliography | 157 |
|     | Index | 159 |

*Other titles in this series include*

BY NEIL LANDS

The Dordogne
Burgundy
Languedoc-Roussillon
Beyond the Dordogne
Brittany

\*  \*  \*

The Auvergne
Northern France (Picardy & Artois)
Eastern France (Alsace, Lorraine, The Vosges)
Provence
Normandy
The Cotswolds
Dorset
East Sussex
West Sussex
Yorkshire
The Lake District
Western Highlands

*Forthcoming titles include*

The Ile de France
Western France (Vendée to Bordeaux)

# Acknowledgements

The Author and publishers would like to acknowledge the assistance of the following people in the writing of this book.

Elfie Tran of the Délégation Pyrénées, Toulouse; Patrick Goyet of Toulouse; Pauline Hallam and Jean Terrieux of the French Government Tourist Office, London; Mlle. Claude Salgues, Directrice Adjoint of the Maison du Tourism, Perpignan; Toby Oliver of Brittany Ferries; Samantha Richley of Normandy Ferries; Linda Groves of Canvas Holidays; Mme. Nogüe of Luz St.-Sauveur; Leonard Gore for his company in Ariège; Paul Traynor for his company on the walk from Carlit to Canigou; and, as always, Estelle Huxley.

*Maps are by Terry Brown*
*All photographs are by the author*

# Illustrations

| | |
|---|---|
| Gotein — a *pelota* match | frontispiece |
| The High Pyrénées | 17 |
| Palace of the Kings of Mallorca, Perpignan | 18 |
| The GR10 | 23 |
| Basque Signpost | 29 |
| Notre-dame du Pont | 31 |
| Compostella door, St Jean | 33 |
| The Nive, St Jean | 35 |
| The 'Pas de Roland' | 37 |
| St Jean de Luz | 40 |
| Louis XIV's Door, St Jean | 41 |
| Biarritz | 42 |
| Early morning in Bayonne | 45 |
| Plaque, Vieux Château | 46 |
| Cloisters, Ste Marie, Bayonne | 47 |
| Church at Gotein | 50 |
| Bridge, Sauveterre de Béarn | 53 |
| Cathedral, Sauveterre | 55 |

Bridge at Orthez                                56
Cathedral of Ste Marie, Oloron                  59
The Saracen pillar, Ste Marie                   60
Tower of Phoebus, Pau                           63
Statue of Henri IV, Pau                         65
The peaks of Bigorre                            71
The Grotto, Lourdes                             73
The Basilica, Lourdes                           75
Church, Luz-St-Saveur                           79
Cirque de Gavarnie                              80
Brêche de Roland                                81
Count Henri Russel                              83
Country near Barèges                            85
Luchon                                          88
Hang-gliding, Superbagnères                     89
Towards the Port de Venasque                    91
Cathedral of St Bertrand                        95
Cloisters, St Bertrand's                        97
The hill of Montségur                          101
The walls of Montségur                         105
Cathar Memorial below Montségur                107
Leper pool, Ax-les-Thermes                     109
Walkers below Mount Carlit                     114
Solar oven, Font Romeu                         117
Pont Séjourne                                  123
St Michel de Cuxa                              127
Hermitage, Notre Dame del Coll                 129
Lintel, St Genis des Fontaines                 131
Church and tower, Collioure                    134
The Castillet, Perpignan                       137
Maillol Statue, Loge, Perpignan                139
Castle of Salses                               143
The Fenouillèdes                               145

14

# 1 · An Historical Introduction

According to Voltaire, Louis XIV once said *"Il n'y a plus de Pyrénées"*, "The Pyrénées are no more". Well, Louis, unlike his contemporary in England, Charles II, was not noted for the accuracy of his remarks and this sweeping statement is more typical of the man than the region.

Marriage, wars and treaties cannot remove the Pyrénées, historically or politically. This unique and beautiful range of mountains is there, etched against the Southern sky, in many ways as enduring a frontier and as little known as they were in the days of the Bourbons, still the dividing line between France and Spain, still the homeland for the Basques and Catalans, and still a challenge to the people from the North. A journey to the French Pyrénées is bound to be different, for this was, so legend has it, the home of the nymph Pyrene, who was seduced by Hercules, and fleeing into the mountains to avoid the wrath of her father, was devoured by bears. The Pyrénées, as you will discover, is a place of legends.

A casual glance at the map would reveal the Pyrénées simply as a mountain range four hundred kilometres long, spanning the neck of land between the Atlantic and the Mediterranean. A closer inspection would show that this first impression is not entirely accurate.

There are, in fact, two separate ranges, the first running from the Atlantic, south and east to the Val d'Aran, the second starting a little north of this gap and completing the distance to the Mediterranean. Through the Val d'Aran the River Garonne flows over into France.

This book is about the French Pyrénées, that part of the range which lies north of the frontier, a line fixed at the Treaty of the Pyrénées in 1659 and which roughly (but with a number of notable exceptions) follows the watershed between the two countries from the Bidassoa to the Cap Cerbère.

The French Pyrénées cover a large and splintered area, seamed with valleys, long mountain walls and deep forests. It is a difficult region to explore, and one which cannot be rushed. I have therefore covered the area by dividing it into its historic provinces and exploring them in turn from the green hills of the *pays* Basque to the dancing plains of Roussillon. As usual, and it is strange to realise that this is my sixth book on provincial France, I have made no attempt to visit every little village and there will be plenty of places 'where the tourists don't go' which the traveller can discover for himself. At the same time I have tried to visit all the main centres and reach them by the lesser known routes so that the larger attractions become pegs to hang the trip on, and the journey is threaded around such centres, rather than tied directly to them. I believe, with Robert Louis Stevenson, that the object of travel is travel, and I travel happily in a land which has history.

\*　　\*　　\*

The Pyrénées, in themselves, have no history, and for much of recorded time contributed no political barrier whatsoever. This is because the frontiers of what we now call Spain lay north of the mountains. Mountains could not support even subsistence farming, and only the passes, which funnelled in trade, gave mountains any value. Trade could be taxed, mountains were useless, the haunt of brigands and, most probably, demons.

The Western Pyrénées belonged to the Kings of Navarre, and

16

*The High Pyrénées*

their subjects, the mysterious Basques. The Kings of Navarre controlled the trade routes into Spain, gaining much income from the pilgrim traffic on the road to Compostella, and sided in turn with the Kings of Castile, France, or England, to maintain their precarious independence. Eventually, after the union of Spain under Ferdinand and Isabella, the four Southern provinces of Navarre were annexed by Spain, but the Northern region maintained itself until Henry of Navarre became Henri IV, King of France, and that as late as 1589.

In the east, in Catalonia, the story is much the same, but this region maintained itself until the Treaty of the Pyrénées in 1659 absorbed Roussillon into the French throne, and fixed the Franco-Spanish frontier to the present line.

\*     \*     \*

*Palace of the Kings of Mallorca, Perpignan*

The Romans colonised Roussillon, and after the usual invasions of Goths and Visigoths, it became a possession of that great prince, the Count of Barcelona, and later of the Kings of Aragon.

In the 14th century, the northern half of Catalonia, Roussillon, the Balearic Islands, the Cerdagne and Montpellier became the fief of the short-lived and ill-fated Kingdom of Mallorca. Perpignan became the capital of this kingdom, and the great red castle of the *"Kings of Majorque"* still dominates the city. There were only three such kings before Pedro IV of Aragon decided to reclaim his ancestral inheritance, and the last King of Majorque died at Crécy in 1346, fighting as a mercenary in the army of France.

The English, in their Hundred Years War with France made few forays into the Pyrénées. The Plantagenets held Bayonne for many years and the Black Prince rode through Roncesvalles on his way to his last victory at Najera, but the enduring marks of the English are very few.

If the two wings of the mountains have had a violent and colourful past the Central Pyrénées are no less historic. Béarn was the birthplace of Henry of Navarre, and supplied much of his army during the long Wars of Religion which tore at France in the 16th century. Bigorre, Comminges and Ariège saw war and glory in the Middle Ages, enduring the endless terror of the Albigensian Crusade, and the rule of the violent and colourful Counts of Foix.

This is a land of high mountains, the Hautes Pyrénées, of castles, legends, tales of witchcraft and the Inquisition, and a thousand little undiscovered places.

Then, on the edge of Roussillon, we will find Andorra, that anachronism which still endures and, through the high Cerdagne, we descend at last to the Mediterranean.

* * *

Before we go any further it would be as well to spend a little time examining the endpaper maps. The Pyrénées are not especially high mountains and the highest peak, the Pic d'Aneto (3404m.) lies in Spain, dominating the Maladeta massif, south of Luchon. On the French side, the high peaks lie in Bigorre, the Pic du Midi d'Ossau (2884m.) being encircled by a series of beautiful jutting crests. These are the Hautes Pyrénées and if they are not particularly high they are remarkably beautiful. Those not yet familiar with the metric system should know that 1 metre = 3.28ft, approximately one yard.

The Pyrénées begin and end with lower hills, and la Rhune (900m) in the Western Basque country is the first noticeable peak. The great peaks over 2000m. begin in Béarn, and many lie in the Balaïtous or within the confines of the Parc National des Pyrénées, a beautiful region said to be the last haunt of the European brown bear. It certainly contains wild boar and many izard, the chamois of the Pyrénées, delightful marmots, and the thankfully rare *desman,* a large aquatic rat. Botanists will adore the Pyrénées, where lilies, lupins, gentian, fritillaries, eidelweiss, crocus, grow wild and in profusion. Bouganvillia and oleander cloak the buildings and lower down the scent of the *maquis* is glorious after rain.

Needless to say, the Pyrénées is great climbing country, well supplied with the huts of the Club Alpin Français. People have been climbing in these hills for centuries, although many peaks are still virtually unknown. Pedro III of Aragon claims to have climbed Canigou in 1280, where he found a dragon living in a lake. When I climbed it, in 1979, both had vanished.

Much of the Pyrénées is granite, a hard and enduring rock, but there is plenty of limestone, with quartz, marble and *schist* in seams among the rocks. Glacier action has formed the northern slopes and carved out many of the *cirques,* and the deep valleys which seam the escarpments. Clouds can gather on the high tops by mid-day, so if you are going out to walk or climb, an early start is advisable.

For the traveller the dominating feature of the Pyrénées is the *col.* A col is a low ridge, or saddle, usually at the head of a valley, or where a ridge or spur running off the main hill flattens out to provide a route across. Our roads in this book lead over many cols, and even in mid-summer they may provide our only·passage, for snow comes early to the Pyrénées and lies late. I have trudged through knee-deep snow in the Cerdagne in October, and seen the *col* du Tourmalet blocked by snow as late as July.

Our route, to stay close to the mountains when not actually among them, will be south of the main West to East highway, the N117, which begins at Bayonne, and does not leave us until Perpignan. Between this road and the crest of the Pyrénées, we will spend our time, and the distance is not great. On the Spanish side, the foothills run many miles out into the plain but here in the north, the distance from plain to mountain top is rarely more than thirty miles.

\*     \*     \*

When to visit the Pyrénées presents no problem for, depending on when you go, this diverse region will always have something to offer. In winter, from Christmas until late April, the higher hills in the Pays Basque, in Bigorre and in the Cerdagne are ski centres, growing yearly in facilities and reputation, yet if you seek an early spring you need look no further.

The valleys of the Basques around Ainhao are green and pleasant, and in Roussillon, *le pays de quatre saisons,* the cherry blossom blooms around Céret by February, and the sun is already warming the red stones in Perpignan.

In Victorian and Edwardian times, even the Sovereign chose to winter in Biarritz, while Pau and Cauterets were famous as spas and winter resorts as far back as the period just after the Napoleonic Wars.

To tour the entire Pyrénées in a short visit would be something of a mistake, and take several weeks of your time. This is a place to visit again and again, and where you go must depend on what you want to do.

The Pyrénées is the place for lovers of the country. Toulouse is the great city of the area, but once in sight of the mountains the towns are small, but very agreeable. Bayonne, Pau, Perpignan, even Lourdes, are well worth visiting. Lovers of the gracious life will feel at home in Cauterets, in Luchon, in Biarritz, in Ax les Thermes, in Bagnères de Bigorre.

Lovers of history must visit St. Jean Pied de Port, Sauveterre de Béarn, Villefranche du Conflent, or the castle country of Ariège, or the Corbières.

In this book, more than in the others, I have found it necessary to abandon my transport and take to my feet, for the Pyrénées is great walking country and there are many places which can only be reached, or only seen at their best, on foot. The great *cirques* of Gavarnie and Troumouse must be visited and the beautiful lakes around the Pic Carlit (2921m) in the Cerdagne, must be seen.

Much of France today is covered by the red and white barred trails of the Grande Randonnée. These, the *Comité National des Sentiers des Grandes Randonnée,* have marked out as footpaths old and new, and two great footpaths traverse the regions of our travels. Coming in from the north is the GR65, *Le Chemin de St. Jacques,* the Road to Compostella, surely one of the most romantic pilgrim roads of all time. We shall meet the GR65, in St. Jean Pied du Port, and in Béarn.

The chain of the Pyrénées is traversed by two footpaths, the GR10, which runs from Hendaye to Banyuls, and the *Haute Route,* which follows the same axis but runs on higher ground. To cover either will take a certain tenacity and several weeks of your time.

Apart from these expeditions there are many local walks, often waymarked by the local Syndicate d'Initiative, and there is no part of the Pyrénées where a certain amount of exploration should not be done on foot. Stout shoes or boots, a rucksack, and a water bottle are essential Pyrénean stores.

\*     \*     \*

Food is always a pleasure, particularly in France and there are few areas which can offer the variety of regional dishes available in

22

*The GR10*

the Pyrénées. An ocean on one side and a sea on the other certainly helps, but the region has many local specialities, and reflects the wide diversity of the inhabitants.

The Basques, like the Catalans, draw their tastes equally from both sides of the range. Their *piperade,* a mixture of tomatoes, peppers, onions, cream and garlic is a dream, and the pigeon of Etchebar, and the veal of Esplette, with onions and ham is worth leaving Ainhoa to experience. In Pau, at the *Le Conté* you can sample the *terrine de coquille St. Jacques au poivre vert,* the duck steaks or *magret,* or *torri béarnais,* a spicey egg soup. Sauce *béarnais,* incidentally, is no product of Pau. It was invented in Paris in about 1830. This is, though, the great place for *poule-au-pot.*

Foix and the Ariège have no great dishes, but the trout and duck are excellent and the little towns shelter some fine restaurants.

Once into Roussillon, regional cuisine is again evident. The *cargolade,* a dish of grilled snails, prepared over an open fire by the men of the village, is the traditional centrepiece of any Catalan celebration, and the little ports along the littoral bring in some fine fish. The *coquille fruit de mer au gratin* or a *matelot de calmar farci,* at the *Bodega* at Collioure are spendid dishes.

In addition Roussillon, which has more than its fair share of good things from the Pyrénées, has good wine.

* * *

The Pyrénées has some shortage of good wine. The Basques have only one of note, *Irouleguy,* which comes from a tiny region around St. Martin de Arrossa.

Irouleguy, red or rosé, is mostly used to enhance the dishes of St. Jean de Luz, and you may have some trouble finding it. Don't worry, incidentally, about the Basque words *Hotx, Hotxa Edam,* on the rosé label. However it sounds it just means "chill before serving".

Béarn has the red Madiran and the *pétillant* whites of Juraçon, from the hills near Pau, and the locals enjoy in addition the "black wine" from Cahors.

Once you arrive in Roussillon though, the wine famine is over for this region below the Cerdagne is awash with wine which, with tourism constitutes the entire local industry. The wines of Roussillon are mostly V.D.Q.S. but the quality is improving steadily so that much of the Côtes du Roussillon is now *appellation contrôlée*. My favourite wines from this area are the reds from Latour de France and the Château de Jau, and for fun, the sparkling *Blanquette de Limoux* from the country south of Carcassonne.

The Corbières have some fine reds, notably the Fitou and the region also produces some notable *aperitif* and *digestif* wines from Banyuls and Rivesaltes. However much you enjoy history, or after a long day in the hills, you may be sure that, when the sun goes down, you need not lack for good things to eat and drink.

\* \* \*

An understanding of a region's history is important to the traveller. It helps the traveller to understand why a land is the way it is and this understanding will take you beyond the mundane matters of living, eating, drinking and enjoying the sights. The spread of the Pyrénées, as we can see, has been lapped by the tides of history, and when they withdraw they leave many traces behind.

The Basques are notably a nation. They have their own language, styles of architecture, traditional customs and religious institutions, and maintain them strongly. The Catalans assemble in every village to dance the *sardane,* and their language is heard accenting even the French tongue, with its heavy word-ends. Visitors used to the clipped French of the north or the long vowels of the Midi may find road directions in Roussillon a little difficult to follow, while in the High Pyrénées, the herdsmen leading their cattle up in the transhumance speak a local patois in *Béarnais* which is known only to themselves.

In 1659, following the successful completion of Cardinal Richlieu's third ambition, which was to give France secure national frontiers, the Spaniards withdrew across the Pyrénées and the present France was complete. The old regions, Basque, Béarn, Roussillon, remained in name only until the Revolution, after which it was decided to sweep away these aristocratic relics and replace them with *départements,* named very often from the principal local river. This is the origin of Ariège, which replaced the *comté* of Foix, and will serve as one typical example.

Today the Pyrénées is spanned on the French side by six *départements,* Pyrénées Atlantiques which embraces the *pays Basque* and Béarn; Hautes Pyrénées which covers Bigorre and Comminges; Haute Garonne which takes in the Couserans; Ariège which covers the former Foix; Aude which, for this book, takes in the Corbières and *pays de Sault;* and finally Pyrénées Oriental, the former Roussillon.

Of course it didn't work! The Basques are still the Basques, and the Catalan claim that nowhere are there . . .

> *Montanyas regalades*
> *Son las del Canigo.*

"Delicious mountains like those of the Canigou", or *No hi la altra terra com la Cerdenya* — "No other land like that of the Cerdagne".

That is Catalan, albeit the sentiments are familiar, so forget the present divisions and see the people and their land as they are, have been, and wish to be.

This then, is your introduction to the Pyrénées, a range of almost infinite variety and uncertain charm. These are mountains and while they are often sunny they can still be harsh. I have seen three metres of snow covering La Pierre St. Martin, and walked over the *col* to Nuria in Spain with rain filling up my boots every half hour. I have been turned back from Tourmalet by snow in July, and been coated with ice on Carlit in October. At such times it is hard to realise why the place is so agreeable. Fortunately memory is a selective thing, and the good times are there to be remembered. In truth, this is a beautiful, exciting place, where the summers are long and the storms short, serving only to add spice and drama to your stay. The great attraction of this area, and my reason for recommending it to you, is its almost infinite variety.

Whatever you wish, here you have a choice. Two oceans, great heights, rolling hills, fertile valleys and plains, deep snows and hot summers, springs when the fruit trees groan under blossom, autumns when the valleys flare with the turning vine leaf, great food and strong wines. Surely when the Catalans say *"No hi alta terra",* they speak for all of it.

26

# 2 · The Pays Basque

Let us begin with the Basques. Although who, exactly, are the Basques? The answer is that nobody really knows. Voltaire replied to this question with a testy, *"The Basques are a little people who dance at the foot of the Pyrénées"* while Victor Hugo, more admiring, said *"The Basques know all of the sea and the mountains"*. Their country, Navarre, was once a kingdom, and even now they make claims to autonomy but, from any standpoint the Basques are different. Their origins were unknown, even to the Romans. Their role in history, if little known, remains significant. The pilot of Columbus' *Santa Maria* was a Basque. Basque shipwrights built the ships of the Armada. Loyola was a Basque. The Basques are travellers and settlers and they can be found as far afield as Nevada and Patagonia, still speaking Basque. The Basque language, *eskuara*, which is widely spoken in the Western Pyrénées, is quite unique. Their architecture, their food, even their games, are peculiar to themselves. The Basque country itself is surprisingly green, misty, beautiful and different, but Voltaire was right in one respect, they do dance, especially the *Fandango*. So, let us begin with the Basques.

I came in from the South, from Roncevalles, down the pass of Val Carlos, how else? Through this winding, rocky defile, rode the

27

paladins of Charlemagne, then Saracen armies heading North to fight against Charles Martel at Poitiers, and later on our own warriors, the Black Prince marching South to the Battle of Najera and, even later, Wellington fighting his way into France with the Peninsula army. During the Middle Ages this road was the path of the Santiago pilgrims. A traveller would need to have no sense of history at all to choose any other route across the frontier. Besides, it leads directly down into St. Jean Pied-de-Port, and there can be no better place to start our travels than in this attractive and historic town.

St. Jean lies in Basse-Navarre, one of the three remaining French provinces of the old Kingdom of Navarre, the other two being Labourd to the west, and Soule to the east, on the border with Béarn. There were originally seven Basque provinces, but when, in 1512, Ferdinand of Aragon drove the Kings of Navarre back across the Pyrénées, the four in Spain theoretically disappeared, although in terms of numbers there are now far more Spanish Basques than French ones.

The origins of the Basques remain obscure, and the normal clue, their language, is no help at all. Rabelais had Panurge speaking Basque! They say that the Devil spent seven years trying to learn it, then gave up in disgust, while York Powell, an authority on the subject and sometime Regius Professor of History at Oxford, states simply, *"Gascon was Latin spoken by the Basques"*. I side with the Devil in this matter and give up!

The Basques or *Vascons* were certainly there before the Romans came and noted, even then, as a hill people devoted to brigandage. As their later history shows, their kings were no mean hands at diplomacy either, sucessfully playing off the more powerful kingdoms to the north and south against each other to maintain their independence. They held land which straddled the frontier and considerable fiefs in France. Charles the Bad, who ruled here in the 14th century, was a great French lord as well as a deadly rival to the neighbouring Count of Foix. The Kings of Navarre kept their dangerous inheritence, if somewhat curtailed after 1512, until as late as 1607, when the Kingdom was united to the French crown, but in the most splendid fashion, for Henry of Navarre became Henri IV of France. If the King of Navarre was a Béarnais by birth and not a Basque, the Basques are prepared to overlook it.

28

*Basque Signpost*

Their language, *Euskara,* seems to have no links with any other European tongue, and to my mind resembles Mexican Aztec or Mayan, studded as it is with all those x's and k's, but it has a pleasant ring to it and is easy on the ear. The Basque language is far more alive than, say, Welsh, and this is remarkable because for hundreds of years their land was flooded with foreign pilgrims on the road to Compostella, none of whom, we may be sure, made any attempt to learn the local language before they finally wound their way through the Santiago gate and arrived in St. Jean Pied-de-Port.

\*       \*       \*

St. Jean is a pleasant little town, red-roofed, and to me anyway, a pleasant surprise. The town of St. John-at-the-Foot-of-the-Pass

29

should, I imagined, be a grim fortress, grey, embattled, set among lowering clouds, but St. Jean is gay, walled of course, but with golden stone, and lively with a cheerful market day crowd.

It was, and is, the capital of Basse-Navarre and the *pays de Aze*. It lies on the River Nive, and for centuries guarded the main gateway south into Spain, or, more often, plugged the Roncevalles gap against invading armies. There were two main passes across the Pyrénées, one at Somport and the other through Roncevalles. Whoever controlled the passes controlled the trade and gained thereby a considerable income.

From about 950 A.D. St. Jean was the focal point for pilgrims heading for the shrine of St. James at Compostella in Galacia, and over the centuries the pilgrim traffic made the little town rich, although it is very small with less than 2000 inhabitants.

After the capture of Jerusalem by the Saracens, and with the difficulties of reaching Rome across the troubled states of Italy, the pilgrimage to Compostella and the shrine of St. James the Elder, *"Sant-Iago"*, was the most meritorious task the virtuous pilgrim or the repentent criminal could undertake. The difficulties in their path were considerable. The first difficulty was to obtain permission and money for the journey. Problems of plague, wars and robbers were just a few of the snags on the way, but a supportive organisation soon grew up which ran right across Europe, largely established on a chain of hospices or monasteries established and run by the monks of the Cluniac Order. The world's first guide book was a guide for Santiago pilgrims, written at Cluny in the 12th century. This guide being in Latin could be understood everwhere, if not by everybody. It is still available, in a French translation, and contains much useful advice about bed-bugs, how to avoid the plague (a daily wash in vinegar is efficacious) with hints on where wearing the pilgrim badge of the scallop shell will avoid payment of bridge tolls, plus hints on the pitfalls that lay in wait on the road to Santiago. All devout Christians went to Santiago and all roads led through St. Jean. The Feast of Santiago is on the 25th July and in the weeks before this day the steady stream of pilgrims would grow to a flood.

The pilgrim would, and still can enter St. Jean through the Porte St. Jacques, and go down through the narrow streets of the Ville Haute. A later Vauban fortress dominates this area today, but the

30

*Notre-dame du Pont*

narrow streets are still evocative of the Middle Ages. Note the door studded with the shells of Santiago, the *coquille de St. Jacques*. Further down lies the Bishop's Prison, where those criminals who preyed on the pilgrims could be locked up to await trial and sentence. The dungeons of the prison still have chains and shackles bolted to the walls, and it must have been a damp grim place when crammed with prisoners.

This road, the Rue de la Citadelle, leads down past the Church of Notre Dame du Pont, our Lady of the Bridge, and the home of St. Francis Xavier who, with Ignace de Loyola, founded the Jesuit Order in the 16th century. The Jesuits were the shock-troops of the Counter Reformation, and Loyola's creed is worth knowing:

*To give and not to count the cost,*
*To fight and not to heed the wounds,*
*To work and never seek to rest,*
*To labour and not ask for any reward.*

No wonder the Jesuits were so successful.

Notre Dame du Pont is fortified and was once a strong point in the ramparts guarding one of several gates into the lower town. The Porte de Navarre goes out directly across the Nive on to the main road, but the Port de France gives more usefully on to the *Hôtel des Pyrénées,* where I had my first Basque meal. I have to confess that I like food, and many Basque dishes are delicious.

Basque food is delicate, interesting, and just that bit different. Try *jambon piperade*, ham in a spicy cheese sauce, which is quite delicious as is *poulet basquaise*, chicken with ham and mushrooms. Trout and crayfish from the Nive are excellent, the latter cooked in white wine and flamed with brandy. Elsewhere, the ham of Bayonne is famous, while the fish and lobsters of the coast are excellent, especially the tuna and *bouillabaisse* from St. Jean du Luz. Try, in Bayonne, the corn-fed chickens of the Landes. In season, the pigeons and ortalons are a rare treat. The one thing the region lacks is a good wine, only Irouleguy being paletable, but it has its own liquer, *Izarra* (or 'star') which comes either green or yellow, and rounds off a meal, although I personally prefer Armagnac.

The road west from St. Jean to the Côte Basque runs across Labourd along the axis of the Nive, through St. Etienne de

*Compostella door, St Jean*

Baïgorry in the Aldudes Valley and up to St. Martin d'Arrossa. This is a region of foothills rather than proper mountains with Jara at 812 metres being the highest peak. The wet Atlantic winds keep the land green and the countryside is lush, although often misty early in the morning. You may imagine, as I did, that a mountain region in the south of France must be arid and bleached dry in summer. This may be true of Roussillon, but is much less so here in the west, where the Atlantic winds bring in an adequate rainfall.

St. Etienne lies in wooded hills, at the foot of the Aldudes Valley, and is notable for its medieval houses, once the homes of the *Cagots,* the Basque 'untouchables'. Like so many things in this region, their origins are obscure, but the Cagots may have originally been lepers. They enjoyed a number of concessions, like freedom from taxation, and the exclusive rights to certain trades, but were totally excluded from local community life. They were forbidden to marry outside their own circle, and although not entirely denied the comforts of religion, they were excluded from religious life even to the extent of having to enter church through their own door.

These *'cagot'* doors are quite a feature of Basque churches, which tend to be large elaborate, well decorated buildings. The gallery is reserved for the male section of the congregation, from which they can keep a watchful eye on their women in the nave below. A certain air of exclusiveness and division seems to permeate the Basques. They have a need to keep themselves apart, and the sense of family and community is very strong. This clannishness is not uncommon in minority communities and, as elsewhere, manifests itself in language and folklore. The Basque tongue is widely spoken, and the people have a care for things historic and *folklorique.*

Basque houses, especially in Labourd and Basse-Navarre, are very interesting with their carved lintels and latticed fronts; solid buildings to endure the weather and the outside world.

From St. Etienne then, west, under the frontier which spans the col at Ispéguy and on across green country through Bidarray — where you should dine at *'Le Pont d'Enfer'* and try the trout — and so to the gorges of the Nive and the *pas de Roland.*

*    *    *

*The Nive, St Jean*

The facts are uncertain, but the legend unshakable, the very stuff of medieval romance. It is rather surprising that Roland and Oliver's story has never been filmed, for it would make quite a good Western.

In the year 778 A.D., the Emperor Charlemagne, having besieged the Moorish strongholds of Saragossa and Pamplona, was withdrawing his army across the Pyrénées, leaving his rearguard and baggage train under the command of the paladin Roland, Lord of the Breton Marches.

From their crags, the Basque mountaineers watched with envy as the army, loaded with booty, wound its way through the defiles below, and when the rearguard, encumbered as it was with all the baggage, eventually fell behind, the Basques attacked in overwhelming force, rolling rocks from the cliffs, slaughtering the soldiers of the rearguard and, in the final rush, killing their leader Roland himself.

From these few facts a *chanson de geste, 'The Song of Roland'*, was written by a troubadour in about the year 1100, and soon swept across Christendom. The Basques became Saracens, the eternal enemies of the Holy Church, and Roland became a giant carving out the great gap of the Breche de Roland with one last sweep of his sword, Durandel, a magic weapon, the handle containing such powerful relics as a tooth of St. Peter and the blood of St. Basil. Blowing his horn three times, with a final blast heard thirty miles away, he bursts the blood vessels in his neck and falls dead, encircled by his foes. Oliver rushes back to his aid, but alas, too late! It is stirring stuff and has provided a theme for poets down the centuries.

*Far off ... a longue haleine,*
*The horn of Roland in the pass of*
*Spain,*
*The first, the second blast, the failing third,*
*And with the third turned back and*
*Climbed once more,*
*The steep road southward, and heard faint the sound*
*Of swords, of horses, the disastrous war,*
*And crossed the dark defile at last and found,*
*At Roncevaux upon the darkening plain,*
*The dead against the dead and on the*
*Silent ground,*
*The silent slain —*

All of which has nothing whatsoever to do with the *pas de Roland* we have here by the Nive, but it's a pretty spot.

Roland fell, if the tale is true, in the pass at Roncevalles but the locals claim that he fell here, kicking a hole, the *pas,* in the rock with one last blow of his mailed foot. Well, why not ...?

Cambo les Bains is a spa, and lies in two parts, half on the hill, half in the Nive Valley. It is a clean pleasant town, a good place to stay, full of those white Labourd houses with wooden shutters and lattice-woodwork painted in the peculiarly Basque colours of deep red, ochre, or forest green.

The Basques take good care of their houses, which are a family possession, descending from generation to generation, rather than from father to eldest son. You will notice that many of them have

The 'Pas de Roland'

have stone lintels carved with the name of the family, their occupation, the date of construction, and often Basque symbols, like their carved swastika, the *Lauburu*.

It is easy to see the attractions of the Basque country from Cambo surrounded by lush valleys and green, green hills. Edmond Rostand, author of *"Cyrano de Bergerac"*, spent years at Cambo, and you can visit his house at nearby Arnaga, but I suspect you will spend more time on the terraces, just looking at the view.

* * *

At Cambo we leave the Nive, at least for a while, and go south towards Esplette, drawn on by the 'great' mountain of La Rhune (900m), which straddles the modern frontier, or by the food available at the *Euzakadi* — notably the *gâteau basque*. Esplette is said — by those who live there — to be the prettiest village in France. It is full of 16th and 17th century houses, and very picturesque.

There are also those who claim, with considerable justification, that this is the true Basque country, and that nowhere will you find villages as pretty as Sare, Ainhoa or Ascain below St. Pée-sur-Nivelle. Take note of the woods hereabouts, for this is the centre for the great Basque pastime, netting, *la chasse a la palombe*. Each Spring and Autumn, vast flocks of pigeons migrate across the Pyrénées and, once caught, every Basque larder is filled with plump birds. Fine nets are suspended in the trees and as the flocks pass overhead the locals spin flat wooden discs high above the birds. The pigeons mistake these discs for hawks and, diving for shelter in the trees, are netted in thousands.

Sare was once, and for all I could learn still is, a great centre for smuggling. Certainly there are many footpaths up and over the Rhune, which make ideal routes for illicit traffic. Pyréneán footpaths were mostly mule trails, and are fairly tough going, but at least clearly marked, and Sare as a walking centre could hardly be bettered.

Sare, with Ainhoe, is outstandingly beautiful and, like many Basque villages has a *pelota* court by the church. I think that the finest court is at Gotein in the Soule, which we will see later, but

38

*pelota* is to the Basques what *boule* is to the *meridional,* so it is worth noting.

A pelota match is very exciting and well worth an evening of your time. There are various versions, *pelota, fronton, jai-alai, trinquet,* played with two or four players, against a wall, as in most villages, or on an open-sided court in the townships. On the larger courts the players wear the *chistera,* (the pelota is the ball) a sort of basketwork glove with which they scoop up the ball and send it hurtling down the court to flash back from the far wall. *Fronton* must be one of the fastest and most athletic ball games in the world, and attracts a passionate audience. At the first *fronton* match I ever attended, in Mexico, I wondered why tennis balls were being tossed about among the audience, only to discover that each contained either money or a betting slip, or both; a split tennis ball being the ideal way of transferring a bet in a terraced audience.

\*      \*      \*

The frontier region is full of little valleys and villages, but let us drag ourselves away from the interior for a while, to see another side of the *vrai vie Basque,* and visit the coast and some of the larger towns along the shore of the Bay of Biscay.

Historically, and even politically since 1659, the River Bidassoa marks the boundary between France and Spain. It has always marked the line between the two Basque provinces of Navarre, in Spain, and Labourd in France, and naturally enough, the river, and especially the little island called the Isle des Faisans at Hendaye has seen its share of history.

Time, they say, washes away all things, and water is equally effective. There is only a little sandspit left to mark the site of this significant island. Here, in 1463, Louis XI met and first debated the partition of Navarre with Henry of Castile. Here, in 1562, Francis I, a prisoner of Charles V since his defeat at the Battle of Pavia, was exchanged for his two sons, and even more significantly, in 1659 it was here on the island that the Kings of France and Spain signed the Treaty of the Pyrénées, which fixed for ever, or at least until now, the frontier between the countries. Political actions apart, brides have been exchanged here, hands

*St Jean de Luz*

firmly and insincerely shaken, the hopes of nations have briefly crystallised on this fly-plagued sandspit.

The political frontier does not apply to the Bidassoa, or indeed to the Bay of Hendaye. Fishing rights to both are shared by the citizens of Hendaye and its Spanish neighbour, Fuenterrabia, each side acting as guardian for six months of the year.

Hendaye itself has survived all this bustle unperturbed. It remains a simple port and a frontier post, the most southern part of the Côte Basque, and a favourite gateway to Spain.

\*    \*    \*

The Côte Basque runs north for a mere twenty miles from Hendaye to the estuary of the Adour below Bayonne. It is a little known stretch of coast, very *touristique,* and quite lovely, with several interesting towns along the way.

40

PORTE FRANCHIE
POUR LE VRAI MARIAGE LE 9 JUIN 1660 PAR
LOUIS XIV ROY DE FRANCE ET DE
NAVARRE ET MARIE THÉRÈSE
D'AUTRICHE INFANTE D'ESPAGNE
PORTE MURÉE APRÈS LA CÉRÉMONIE
CÉLÉBRÉE DEVANT JEAN D'OLCE D'INCLEY
ÉVÊQUE DE BAYONNE

*Louis XIV's Door, St Jean*

*Biarritz*

Low cliffs mark the *corniche* from Hendaye to Ciboure. Here in former times stood the watchtowers, the *atalayas* of the whalers. The Bay of Biscay once swarmed with whales on which the Basques preyed most profitably, until the whales, which are intelligent creatures, saw fit to take themselves off to temporary safety elsewhere.

The same might be said of the Cagots who lived in some numbers

in Ciboure, until dispersed in the witch-hunts which plagued the Basque country in the 17th century. The musician Ravel was born here, and Ciboure has flourished and declined in tune with the fortunes of its rival, St. Jean de Luz, just across the water.

St. Jean on the River Nivelle, was once a whaling port, and is still a great centre for fishing, notably for tuna and anchovies, catches of this latter fish amounting on occasion to 400 tons a day, which would cover a large amount of toast! It is also quite fashionable and a tourist centre. The rooftops are dominated by the Church of St. Jean Baptiste, where Louis XIV married his much neglected queen, after collecting her on that island in the Bidassoa. After the couple left the church, the doorway was walled up so that no *ordinary* couple could share the privileges of the Roi Soleil. The more you learn about Louis XIV, the more destestable he becomes! Who else could remark, after losing to Marlborough at Malplaquet *"Has God then forgotten all I have done for him"!* or on another occasion *"I very nearly had to wait"!*

St. Jean is an agreeable resort, with many fine buildings in the *Quartier de la Barre,* near the port, and a foretaste of the regal charms of Biarritz further to the north.

*   *   *

Like many popular places, Biarritz has seen better days. Emperors and Empresses, Kings with their Queens, courtiers and *poules des luxes* once made this place their mecca. On a more prosaic level it resembles Bournemouth and is notable today for surfing and some excellent restaurants, especially the *Café de Paris* in the Place Bellevue.

The main part of the town stands on a little headland, the Atalaye, with a rocky reef, the Virgin's Rock, leading out to the sea. This spur is flanked on either side by two surfing beaches, the *grande plage,* and the *plage des Basques,* with smaller beaches tucked between the rocks. The great rollers sweep in here from the Atlantic and give Biarritz a reputation as the best surfing centre in Europe, some compensation perhaps for the loss of former glories.

The Empress Eugenie, wife of Napoleon III, made Biarritz famous. She found it a familiar echo of her native Spain, and persuaded her husband to built a house there. Our own Prince of Wales, later Edward VII, loved all things French, and having once visited Biarritz at the Empress's request, came again frequently, until shortly before his death. Indeed, so strong a hold did the town exert, that when Asquith became Prime Minister in 1908, Edward VII, who was on holiday there, declined to come home so that Biarritz has witnessed the only occasion a British Prime Minister has kissed hands for his appointment on a foreign soil.

*Early morning in Bayonne*

Today, well, it is different. There are casinos and a museum full of nasty fish. It is still lovely, although it has come down in the world. The streets are full of sea-bleached youngsters carrying surf boards, the town has some excellent restaurants, and it is still fashionable to stay in the great hotels. If it seems a little sad, well then, that could just be my imagination.

*　　*　　*

On every trip, and I almost said in every region, you will find a place that makes the whole trip worth while — if for that place alone. Frequently, the place you like is the one you least expect to. For me, on this trip, Bayonne, sparkling, clean, chic Bayonne is just such a place. Wherever else you visit, visit Bayonne to enjoy the true heights of French provincial charm. It stands on the Adour, where that frontier river dividing the *pays Basque* from Béarn is joined by the Nive, which we left behind at Cambo.

Bayonne has great style, and is the main port for the *pays Basque* and Béarn. On a more prosaic note it is famous for ham and chocolate. For centuries it belonged to the English Kings, and their

*Plaque, Vieux Château*

*Cloisters, Ste Marie, Bayonne*

Plantagenet arms still glow in the cathedral glass, but the French General, Dunois, Bastard of Orleans, and companion of Joan of Arc, captured it in 1451. Later on it was fortified by Vauban and built on and added to by Louis XIII and XIV. It is now a classic example of the French provincial town.

Bayonne is vaguely remembered as the town which gave its name to that symbol of the *furia française,* the bayonet, when a Bayonne regiment, running out of ammunition during some skirmish in the Seven Years War, tied their daggers to their muskets in lieu of pikes, and drove the enemy back. Bayonne has a long history as a centre for the manufacture and trade in arms and armour, so this feat of arms is a typical manoeuvre.

The town has several places worth a visit, notably the Vieux château, old enough to have Roman foundations and where just about everybody seems to have stayed, from the Black Prince onwards, and the great cathedral of Ste. Marie. This has enormous cloisters and is a vast cathedral, full of medieval glass, registering the arms of England and of the Talbot family, marshals to Henry VI. Note the knocker on the north door which, if he could grasp it, gave life to a fleeing thief. Sanctuary knockers are very rare, and

47

this one seems well worn, as are the cloisters, although they have antiquity as their excuse.

I am not a great lover of museums, which often seem to be dead places, but the Musée Basque, across the Nive in Bayonne, is fascinating. Firstly, it gives a real insight into a land and people that are truly and significantly different. Room after room records the history of the Basques, and explains all their symbols by which they declare and affirm their unique identity. Note, for example, the blazon of chains on a red field, recalling the time when, at the battle of Las Navas Tolosa in 1212, the Basque contingent shattered the bodyguard of the Sultan Miramolin who, confident of victory, had chained themselves together. This coat of arms links together the Basques of Navarre on both sides of the frontier. One room is entirely devoted to examples of the Basque swordstick, the *makhila,* a long staff of carved wood, steel and leather. If you want to buy one you will have to go to Larressore, near Sare. Another contains countless examples of the *linge basque*, the local needlework, which outside the museum you will find in use at many restaurants.

Finally, if this diet palls, there is a room devoted to sorcery and witchcraft, in which the Basques were once said to be skilled. The Inquisition carried out several purges in the area. Even Henry IV, a notably tolerant monarch, saw reason to send his investigators to Bayonne, and the burning of witches here continued until well into the 17th century. This museum is a real living collection and well worth an afternoon of your time. After all, the sun will shine tomorrow.

Out again, for dinner at the nearby *La Tanière* restaurant, then on around the ramparts as the evening falls. Later on stroll to one of the many pavement cafes near the cathedral. Stay a little in Bayonne and explore the region round about, for I like it, and so will you.

\*     \*     \*

I am reminded that we are here to see the Pyrénées and stand now on the border of the Landes. We still have to travel the eastern marches, and the still unvisited region of Soule.

South then, towards Béarn, and if we swing back again to the frontier of Béarn later, then we have the plea of logic, since most travellers will approach the Pyrénées from the north.

Bidache is a castle town, set in the hills. The English fought the Basques here and, so they say, were painfully defeated. This may be, although the facts are obscure but, to return to the Santiago road, where we began this chapter, let us press on to St. Palais. The Compostella Pilgrims from Bordeaux, including therefore many English, came down through St. Palais, and left their mark here on the church and in the chapel of St. Nicolas in nearby Harambels. This is interesting, for considering the volume of traffic, the pilgrims have left little trace of their passing, few statues, few carvings. You have to look closely to realise that half Christendom passed this way, but this road leading through from Sauveterre south through St. Palais to St. Jean is the original Compostella road.

To the west, between St. Palais and Hasparren lie the great caves of Oxocelhaya, and although I am not given to ferreting about in the depths of the earth, it must be mentiond that the Pyrénées are famous for their caves and a delight for spelaeologists.

These particular grottos date back in occupation to the paleolithic period, as do those in the Dordogne, and are similarly decorated with carvings and cave paintings, although the quality cannot match that at Lescaux.

Below St. Palais, still on the road to Compostella, lies Larcevcau, marked by the red and white splashes of the G.R.65, and here we turn east over the col d'Osquich towards Mauleon.

If you want to get lost in the *pays Basque* and find a place *'where the others don't go'*, then anywhere south of this little road will suit you very well. You will have to go on foot, since roads are few or non-existent, but in the hills of Arbailles, which separate Navarre from Soule, or in the region around the chapel of St. Anthony, you can be truly alone, and a trek to the knife-like gorges of Kakouetta can be a real adventure.

These hills, an echo of the High Pyrénées, which periodically emerge from the clouds to nod a distant greeting, are not particularly high, running up to no more than 1100 metres, but the views they offer are spectacular and the hills are green, while the Pic d'Orthy at 2017 metres overlooks the scene.

*     *     *

*Church at Gotein*

The Soule is a well-bred country, a mixture of Basque and Béarnais, but perhaps because dilution is a constant danger, a famous place for Basque dances, plays and folklore, and not without its history. Aramits, a glittering whitewashed village on the eastern border is said to be the home of Dumas's musketeer Aramis, and if it looks too new, this is because the old village was destroyed in an earthquake in 1968 and has only just been rebuilt.

Gotein, near Mauléon, has that classic Basque church, with frontier court, cagot entrance, gallery for the menfolk, and all in excellent preservation, the one Basque church you have to see. Mauléon is a busy town with a fine château-fort and is the capital of the *pays de Soule.* Now it makes shoes, those ankle searing thonged sandles, the *espadrilles,* waits for tourists, and hopes for better days.

\*    \*    \*

We have almost run out of the Basque country, although there is enough there in a hundred little valleys to keep you here for years, at a slower pace, or bring you back again constantly.

To sum up the charm of the Basque country in a sentence is fairly simple. It is green, clean and historic. The Atlantic winds contribute to the former, and the Basques pride in their country ensures that nothing is destroyed or spoiled which could be preserved by some little effort.

Apart from all those obvious points, the Basques are different. Somehow or other they have maintained their identity in that curious splintered kingdom, since before recorded history, and are still united and unique. That takes a little doing, but they have managed it and when you cross the river into Béarn you know you have left something special behind.

# 3 · Béarn

The frontiers of the Basque country are curiously unmarked. You pass along and one minute you are in a Basque village, complete with pelota court and carved lintels, and the next moment you are in Béarn. There are few geographic divisions to the east and the boundaries are more cultural than topographic, in spite of the Atlantic and the looming Pyrénées.

The exception to this is in the north, for the land between the two rivers, the *gave* d'Oloran and the *gave* de Pau is clearly a march, an ancient war zone, buttressed as usual with *bastides,* those small, delightful, fortified towns of the 13th and 14th centuries. You can often spot a *bastide* by its name, for they are usually called Villefranche, Villeneuve, Sauveterre, Villereal or some such title, and our first, Le Bastide Villefranche on the *gave* d'Oloran is a typical combination and obviously of French construction, erected, no doubt, against the perfidious Plantagenets. This town has the usual fortifications, a donjon overlooking narrow *bastide* streets, and is a foretaste of the beauty waiting a little upstream, at another but much larger *bastide,* Sauveterre de Béarn.

This town is built on a bluff overlooking the river and still retains many of the medieval fortifications including a fine Romanesque

*Bridge, Sauveterre de Béarn*

church, and the remains of a fortified bridge in the river below. From that bridge in 1170 Sancia, wife of Count Gaston of Béarn, was tried by ordeal. She had been accused of murdering her son by witchcraft and, hands and feet tied together, she was thrown into the river and promptly sank. Had she floated her witchcraft would have been proved, but with that problem solved the lady's life was still in danger until the swift current washed her up on the far shore. One cannot imagine that hurling your wife in the river does much for marital bliss thereafter!

Sauveterre is a good place to start our tour of the vast and varied province of Béarn, for it stands at the northern junction of three ancient provinces, Navarre and the *pays Soule,* the domain of the English in Aquitaine to the North, and across the river to the East, the Comté of Béarn. Sauveterre drew its former importance from this fact. Its strategic importance vanished in 1462 when Louis XI annexed the Northern provinces of the Counts of Foix, but the town is still beautiful and has very well preserved medieval fortifications. Gaston VII of Foix built the castle, and Gaston Phoebus enlarged it, and died here after a fall while hunting. If you stay at the Logis hotel, *A Baste,* you can enjoy good food, and explore the castle and the adjoining Romanesque church at leisure. The castle dates from the eleventh century, and was completed by Gaston VII who built the Tower Moncade at our next stop, Orthez.

The road to Orthez goes either through Salies, which is pleasant but unremarkable, or you can follow the minor road through l'Hopital d'Orion, on the Compostella trail and pass the lovely church of Burgaronne on the way. You will see the waymarks of the GR65 all along this route, once followed by English pilgrims from Bordeaux.

\*     \*     \*

Orthez is famous for its bridge. Like the one in Sauveterre it is fortified, but in this case it is still complete, spanning the *gave* de Pau in a series of fine arches. Orthez was once the capital of Béarn. Gaston Phoebus lived here and held a glittering court in the Tour Moncade. This dates from 1242 and is all that remains of his palace. It was in the dungeon of the Tour Moncade that Gaston Phoebus accidentally murdered his son. The boy had been on a

*Cathedral, Sauveterre*

*Bridge at Orthez*

diplomatic visit to that notorious rogue, Charles the Bad, King of Navarre and returned bringing with him a box of sweetmeats as a present for his father, which Charles had previously poisoned. This was somehow discovered, and Gaston, who, although a good lord, was unusually suspicious, hanged his son's retinue and imprisoned the boy in the castle cellars. There, in his rage, he thrust a dagger at his son's throat and accidently severed an artery, through which, unseen in the dark and still silent the boy bled to death.

Orthez saw more bloodshed during the Wars of Religion, when the Protestant mercenary captain, Montgomery, a Scot no less, took the town and forced the Carmelite nuns to jump into their

own well, while the monks from the Cordelier monastery were thrown from the walls into the river. If you feel you have had enough of this a meal at the *Château des Trois Poètes*, will restore you. This dates from 1600, and has welcomed Vigny, Lamartine and Jammes, hence the name.

Except for the ruins and the bridge Orthez is not a place that need detain us long on our road back to the high Pyrénées.

Navarrenx, on the gave d'Oloron, sounds as if it should be Basque, but it is well within Béarn. It produces a palatable wine and is a great centre for salmon fishing and was once a *puissant bastide,* commanding the valley above Oloron.

\*    \*    \*

Oloron-Ste-Marie on the other hand is a fine city. It stands at the point where the *gave* d'Aspe and the *gave* de Ossau, flowing in from their respective valleys join to form the wider *gave* d'Oloron. The town is a network of narrow streets and humped bridges, dividing the town into two areas, each with its great church, the *quartier* Sté Croix, and the *quartier* Sté-Marie. In the former stands the excellent *Hôtel de Béarn* which is worth staying at not just for the comfortable rooms and fine cuisine, but for the excellent collection of paintings and weapons that adorn the walls.

Oloron, like Orthez, was once the capital of the Viscount of Béarn, and now lives, rather like Bayonne, by manufacturing chocolate. It was founded in Roman times by Publius Crassus, son of the man who fought Spartacus and was killed by the Parthians. It grew rich in the Middle Ages for it controls the route down to and from the pass at Somport. From Ste. Croix, or rather the promenade which encircles it, you get your first glimpse of the High Pyrénées, snow-capped even in July, and you can see just across the river, the towers of the cathedral of Ste. Marie. This was built about 1120 by Gaston IV, Vicomte de Béarn, who had ridden in the First Crusade and taken part in the siege and capture of Jerusalem. The porch and typanum records, as usual, the events of the Apocalypse, watched from the side by a mounted statue of the Vicomte himself, while the central pillar is supported by a carving of two chained Saracens, a reminder to his vassals of the Vicomte's

58

*Cathedral of Ste Marie, Oloron*

*The Saracen pillar, Ste Marie*

prowess in the Holy Land. It is a very fine piece of work, and the marble has been eroded and polished until it has the lustre of ivory.

As it stands at a river junction, we have a choice of routes in Oloron, and to try each, it is south now, to Aramits on the edge of the *pays de Soule*, and on to Arette. This area was devastated by an earthquake in 1968, so most of the buildings are very new, but not so new as the resort of La Pierre St. Martin high up on the frontier. This is a modern ski resort, and I have been there when it floundered under three metres of snow, and we thought we were there until spring. Even in July there is snow on the tops, and on July 13th every year the farmers of Arette meet with their neighbours from the Spanish side, up on the *col,* and exchange tokens of friendship and confirm their rights to common grazing which date back to the 14th century. Their pacts is re-sworn every year with a handshake across the *mont joie,* or pile of stones which mark the frontier at the col. Apart from the skiing the region around La Pierre St. Martin is a notable place for caving with many great caverns in the immediate vicinity.

Below La Pierre St. Martin, a minor forest road leads east, winding through the forests and up to the Col de Houratate. Our road often leads across these *cols* or passes, and if the snow lies late on the hills they may prove impassable.

Bedous on the *gave* d'Aspe is a good centre for touring south into the valley of the Aspe up to Somport and then across into Spain and into the National Park of the Pyrénées. This region is best explored on foot for the roads are few, but the valley of the Aspe is beautiful, a sharp gorge, knifing into the mountains.

Above the hills, to the east, the Pic du Midi d'Ossau rears up at 2884 metres, and can be reached along the GR.10 from the gorges at Pointe d'Enfer. Tall peaks mark out the frontier on either side as you follow the valley of the Aspe up to the tunnel at Somport, for the Aspe like the Garonne rises in Spain.

*     *     *

North of Bedous lies the superb little village of Sarrance, a stop on that other road to Compostella which leads over the Somport pass. There is a much restored 13th century cloister in the old church. The *Hôstellerie de St. Jacques* just down the road is a fine place to eat on a wet and windy day, with great hams drying in the wide fireplace. It serves Béarnais specialities and stands on the site of an old *hospice.*

At Escot, if the *col* de Marie Blanque is open, we turn east on a minor road through the forest of Escot, over the *col* and out into the delightful country of the Benou. Once past the little chapel of Our Lady of Houndass, you emerge into a valley so quiet and picturesque that it looks like a painting. Fat cattle and sparkling sheep browse on the lush grass, while gorse flames on the open rock-studded moors. Water trickles everywhere across the stony beds of the streams, and all this peace and beauty is just a short distance from the main road that links Pau to Laruns in the valley of the Ossau.

Decisions, decisions, is there no escape? One of the problems with travel in the Pyrénées is the necessity to retrace one's steps, something I prefer to avoid whenever possible. However, in a region which largely consists of steep valleys, boxed in by mountains, some doubling back can hardly be avoided, so it must be south first to Laruns and into the valley of the Ossau, overshadowed by the loom of the Pic itself.

This is country for the skier and the hill-walker with ample accommodation at Artouste for wandering in the Sagette, or up the valley to the lakes which lie below the north-west face of the Pic du Midi d'Ossau. You are getting into the high hills now, so a degree of caution is advisable.

This is wonderful scenery, the green of forests, white snowcaps on the high peaks, with deep lakes reflecting the blue of the sky. You could stay here for days camped beside the road or wandering along paths through the hut network of the *Club Alpin Français* within the National Park. Camping itself is not, in theory anyway, permitted within the Park, but the huts are plentiful. A pause then, in this fine country, but this is Béarn and we must now go north to Pau, the present capital of Béarn and the city of Henri IV.

\*      \*      \*

Pau is a magnificent provincial city, with great style. It was the birthplace of Henry of Navarre, Henri IV of France, the Vert-Galant, he of the white plume, and the *poule-au-pot,* countless

*Tower of Phoebus, Pau*

mistresses and stout-hearted friends, who declared that *'Paris was worth a Mass',* established religious toleration with the Edict of Nantes, and is, without a doubt, the most popular monarch in French history.

Henri was the grandson of Henry II of Navarre, Vicomte de Béarn, and Marguerite d'Angouleme, a sister of François Premier. When the Valois kings bred out down to their last unfortunate Henry III, the Catholic North realised that the heir to the throne was the great-nephew of Francois I, the Protestant Prince of Navarre. Navarre had turned Protestant after the conversion of Henri's mother, Jeanne d'Albret who was married to Anthony de Bourbon, a descendent of the sixth son of St Louis.

63

The Wars of Religion devastated France throughout the 16th century and had Henry IV done no more than bring them peace, that would have been enough, but Henry was the perfect king for the French. I bow to no one in my love for things French and admire a people who can appreciate their inheritance, but it cannot be said that they are an easy people to live with. Compromise is not the French way, they have to be led and, however reluctantly, they admire a firm hand.

Henry of Navarre was a good leader, and like all such, he led from the front. He wore a great white plume on his helmet in battle *"so that all may know where the King fights and may thereby follow him"*. He was compassionate, and no ruler, certainly no Bourbon, ever expressed more concern for his poorest subjects with the simple thought that *"every peasant had the right to a chicken in his stew pot (poule-au-pot) every Sunday"*. That was a lot in the 16th century, but it is curious how the simple wishes live on and are remembered after the ringing speeches are forgotten.

The French admired, and still admire the King's logic, with his "Mass for Paris", when he became a Catholic to end the Wars. They also remember that on doing so he kept faith with his Protestant supporters, signing the Edict of Nantes which brought peace to France for many years, until it was trimmed by Richlieu and then revoked by Louis XIV.

*     *     *

This then is something of the man who was born in the great castle at Pau to the sound of Béarnais folk songs sung by his mother during labour, and later rocked to sleep in the great turtle-shell cradle they still keep there.

The castle itself was a medieval fortress, the main tower, in brick, being built by Gaston Phoebus. The original castle was much altered and enlarged by Henry's father about 1530, and is now a Renaissance château on almost classic lines. You enter across a dry moat and into a courtyard, inspected as you pass by a fine statue of the great king.

The castle contains the Musée du Béarnais and, although I am no lover of museums, this one, as with that of the Basques at Bayonne, is worth a visit so that the history of this region and its people may

*Statue of Henri IV, Pau*

be quickly appreciated. Moreover, since much of Béarn is outdoor country, here is the place to learn about the local flora and fauna, from the wide range of natural history exhibits.

The rooms of the castle are beautifully furnished with Gobelin tapestries, paintings, armour and furniture, all well cared for, while from the terraces you can see across the river to the distant Pyréneès, the perfect backdrop to the town. Lamartine said that the view of the mountains from the Boulevard des Pyrénées in Pau could only be compared for beauty with the sea view of Naples, and on a clear day he may be right.

Pau, apart from being a good centre for touring Béarn, must be a pleasant place to live, and besides Henry IV has had its share of famous sons, notably the Napoleonic general Bernadotte, who eventually became King of Sweden. Jean-Baptiste Bernadotte was born in Pau in 1760 and by 1784 was a general in Napoleon's army. He became a Marshal of France, and when he was sent to Stockholm bearing some Imperial demand he so impressed the Swedes with his tact that they later asked him if he would care to become their king. Unless, of course, he was too busy! Needless to say, Bernadotte dropped Napoleon like a hot brick, made a rapid switch from Catholicism to Calvinism and became Crown Prince of Sweden, where his descendents rule to this day.

Our own no-less-lucky general, Wellington, came this way in 1814, marching north to end the penultimate phase of the Napoleonic Wars at Toulouse, and Pau later became a recreation centre for his officers, who, once the Wars were over, returned to Pau in large numbers with wives and families so that until 1914 the town housed a considerable British colony, and catered for it with horse races, fox hunting, and all the traditional entertainments of the English gentleman, including rugby, which still dominates the sports fields of South-Western France. Today, Pau has a population of about a hundred thousand, many good hotels, and several fine restaurants. Try the *saumon frais au Juraçon,* local fish with local wine and you can really taste the pleasures of the town, or for something more exotic, Vietnamese food in the *Lotus d'or* while the little *Chez Moxim's* near the château is perfect for lunch.

\*    \*    \*

Beyond the walls of Pau lies the vineyards of Juraçon, the finest wine, in my opinion anyway, in the Western Pyrénées. They say that when Henri IV lay in his tortoise-shell cradle at Pau his lips were moistened with a clove of garlic and sips of wine from Juraçon, the clove for health, the wine for wit and political craftsmanship. The mixture obviously worked.

The vineyards of the region were destroyed by the phylloxera pest at the end of the last century and only began a major recovery after the Second World War, a Renaissance which started, appropriately enough, with the replanting of the vineyards around the village of Gan, about five miles south of Pau. I say 'appropriately' because Gan was the birthplace of Henri IV's most enduring mistress *'La Belle Corisande'*, a lady who so captivated the King that he abandoned the fruits of his victory at Coutras in 1588, and hurried back to Pau to lay the captured standards of the Catholic League at her feet.

Juraçon is a curious place for a good wine. The vineyards are at over 300 metres and often covered thickly with snow in the winter. Their area is not large, and most of the wine should be drunk young, say after six months, so the current vintage, and the vintage is late in Juraçon, often taking place in November, can be drunk the following summer. Juraçon wines are whites or rosé, while a little further to the north are the full red wines of Madiran, where there are even some pre-phylloxera vines. The older reds can take years to mature and are at their best when eight to ten years old. The vineyards of Madiran were originally established by monks from Burgundy, and since the wine is both full and fruity, like a good Burgundy, there may be some virtue in this. Whatever the origin, you will find that a Juraçon, well chilled, will go with your trout or salmon from the *gave* du Pau, while Madiran complements your *filet mignon avec sauce béarnaise,* which last, I have to tell you, has nothing to do with Henri IV and was only invented at St Germain near Paris in the mid-19th century. Another illusion shattered!

*       *       *

Pau is an excellent centre for touring Béarn with good communications in every direction. You can get complete guidance from the Tourist Office at the *Parlement de Navarre* in the Rue Henri IV in Pau. One popular visit is to the caves at Bétharram, on the borders of Bigorre. This vast subterranean network was discovered by shepherds in 1819 and slowly explored for the rest of the 19th century, by which time many miles of caves had been uncovered.

It is a huge grotto, hollowed out by a river which eventually flows out into the *gave* de Pau, and a chilly visit takes over an hour to complete. On emerging you should also visit the sanctuary of Our Lady of Bétharram, a shrine built in the late 17th century at about the time of the Catholic revival in the mainly Protestant South-West, an event which took place some years before Louis XIV revoked the Edict of Nantes and drove many Huguenots into exile.

\*     \*     \*

From Bétharram you can head south and west across country on minor roads to the valley below Pau, and towards Bielle. The country to the south is hilly now and, as you will soon see, a cattle range, backed by the snow caps of the Massif around the Pic du Midi d'Ossau.

We stand now on the edge of the High Pyrenees, where the *transhumance* has been a way of life for centuries. The *transhumance* is found in many mountain areas where the pasturing of sheep or cattle is dictated by the snow line, and since the local people live as herdsmen or shepherds it affects them as well.

Much of the true pasture lies high up in the hills, well above the tree line, so that in the Spring, as the snow retreats, the cattle are herded out of their winter byres, and plod up, in steady herds, to fatten on the high grass. Their owners, perforce, come with them and spend the summer following their herds around the mountains. The cattle themselves are fine, lethargic beasts, many equipped with large bells which render the far-famed peace and tranquillity of the mountains a complete illusion. The hills reverberate to the clamour of cattle bells, and when they gather outside your tent in the misty morning, moo-ing and jangling, you may think that *anywhere* must be quieter than this.

68

South of Laruns the road runs south round the Pic de La Sagette, and along the lake to the Pont d'Arrious, starting place for some excellent walks on the axis of the GR.10.

To the West, the path leads up to the Pombie hut and from here a fit walker on a fine day (note the stipulations) can circle the Pic du Midi d'Ossau, in about eight hours. To the east lies the Lac d'Artouste and the way into the remote lake district of the Balaïtous, straddling the frontier, while, further south again, the col du Pourtalet leads over into Spain.

Eaux-Bonnes, east of Laruns, is a spa. There are many such spas in the Pyrénées and we will meet them increasingly as we go east. Each has its specific, and Eaux-Bonnes specialises in the treatment of bronchial ailments, but on a more vigorous note is a great walking centre, and a starting point for climbing in the Pic de Ger.

From Eaux-Bonnes, a winding route leads up and up to the resort at Gourette, a ski-centre perched on an escarpment with a silver waterfall arcing into the valley, a bustling place in winter and, at present anyway, dead as a doornail in summer. This will change because Gourette is the perfect centre for summer hill walking and climbing activities, tucked into the high hills under the *col* d'Aubisque, which is reached after a steady climb to stand at last on a windy hill, with the great hills of the Hautes-Pyrenées all before us. This is one of the highest cols, at 1700 metres, so the view are spectacular. The wind sighs, the eagles soar, and the cattle gallop off with a mighty din. This is spectacular country, magnificent scenery and splendid views across wide valleys and snow capped peaks.

This road, from Aubisque down to Arrens, is one of those routes not to miss when touring in the Hautes-Pyrénées. The road itself is fantastic, hanging limpet-like along the edge of the ravines, with steep cliffs falling away below, first on one side and then on the other. If the *col* is open this is the road to take.

Once over the *col* we leave Béarn behind, and enter the comté of Bigorre to descend through this wonderful landscape to the valley of Cauterets and so to Lourdes.

# 4 · Bigorre

When you think of the Pyrénées proper, of high mountains, rushing torrents, fields full of flowers, the great walls of the *cirques*, then you are probably thinking of Bigorre. This ancient region, known to Caesar, is now enveloped by the *départment* of the Hautes-Pyrénées, and all the main natural marvels of the range are to be found within these boundaries.

An eagle circling the peaks above Bigorre would look down on a pear-shaped province, the stalk at Lourdes and Tarbes, widening out across Arglès-Gazost and Bagnères de Bigorre, and rounded out at the base by the frontier that swings round to the east from the Balaïtous massif to Vignemale through Gavarnie and so into the eastern province of Comminges over the *col* de Peyresourde.

It is difficult to get into the Balaïtous region. Like so much of the more remote Pyrénées, it can only be explored on foot, although access is possible from the Vallée d'Ossau. A number of minor roads run into it from Bigorre up the Vallée d'Arrens, or even from the Pont d'Espagne above Cauterets and then through the Pyrénean National Park, of which the remote Balaïtous forms a major part. The *Parc National des Pyrénées* was established in 1967 to protect the habitat and wildlife of the region. It is now linked to

*The peaks of Bigorre*

the reserve at Néovielle, and abuts the Spanish reserve of Ordesa across the frontier.

The reserve is about 106 kms. in length, and varies in width from 5 kms. to 16 kms. It contains hundreds of miles of footpaths, and over 250 lakes, and in this vast and varied habitat the wildlife thrives. There is bear, perhaps, and izard, the Pyrenean chamois certainly, pine-martin, marmots, eagles and vultures, and the curious *desman*, a large water-rat with a long nose and webbed feet, which, thank goodness, I have yet to meet. But flora and fauna apart, the glory of the range is its mountains.

Vignemale is the highest peak on this part of the frontier at 3298 metres, but the whole region is a mass of lakes and parks, crossed by the GR.10, and really well supplied with C.A.F. huts. It is said that some of the last bears to roam free in Europe can be found in the Balïtous, although sightings seem extremely rare, to say the least. I have asked scores of people and none of them have ever seen a bear though all maintain that they are there.

Coming east, over the *col* d'Aubisque, all these spectacular mountains lie to the south. Below Arrens lies the picture-postcard village of Bun, which gives wonderful views back towards the Pic de Ger and the Gabizos, two peaks which mark the boundary with Béarn and, through the Vallée d'Arrans, a brief glimpse of the distant Balaïtous. The *Hôtel au Relais du Col* at Bun is a good centre for exploring this region, and Aucun, nearby, has a beautiful church with a fine bell tower.

From Bun you can get up to the lac d'Estaing and towards Mount Né (2724m), which divides the valley from Cauterets, which can be reached on the GR.10.

*   *   *

It is so easy to be engulfed by the scenery in the Pyrénées that you forget the people, and this would be a pity for their history is interesting.

Bigorre and Tarbes were mentioned by Caesar in his *'Commentaries'* as a spa, while Tarbes was then and is still the commercial centre for the region. The *Bigourdans* were even then a hardy people, and the mountaineers of the Lavedan, living in their seven valleys around the frontier peaks, maintained their independence throughout the Middle Ages, having made a pact with their Count, which stated that their rights, mainly the right to be left alone, took precedence over his, and that they would pay him homage only for as long as he respected their rights. This set fuedalism on its head, but it seemed to work. Neither did the Salic Law apply in the Pyrénées. Women could and did inherit countries and kingdoms, Jeanne d'Albert being a good example, but when they or any lord tried to exercise their rights, the locals often reacted firmly. Tax collecting was one occupation fraught with hazard, and the *gabelle,* or salt tax was never collected hereabouts. At Argelés Gazost, one tax collector was given a patient hearing, then conducted to a nearby peak and thrown off the top! This peak is still called the *Saute du Procurer.* You can see that the *Bigourdans* are one of *us* rather than *them!*

72

The *comté* belonged to the English from 1360 to 1406, when it came into the possession of the Counts of Foix and so eventually into union with Béarn and Navarre and finally going French, but only as late as 1607.

Below Lourdes, which was a medieval stronghold long before it became a religious centre, lie the 'Seven Valleys of the Lavedan', the true high mountains, and here is the delightfully named *pays Toy.* Bigorre, like the rest of the range is full of *'pays'*, usually taking their name from the local river, or rather from the local name *for* a river.

For example, we have had the *pays de Gave,* and as we have seen already, *gave* is the name *for* a river, or more properly, a torrent, rather than the name *of* a river. Here, just to confuse you, it is different again; we have the *pays. The pays de Neste, the pays de Gave,* records a river, but just to be different, the Barronies is a district. However, let us leave the valleys for a little while and go north across the plain to Lourdes.

\*     \*     \*

*The Grotto, Lourdes*

Lourdes is dominated by a massive medieval fortress. The former castle was once held by the Moors and once besieged by Charlemagne. The present castle should be your first stop, for it contains a Musée Pyrénées, which will give you a useful insight into the regions we are about to visit. This museum was organised by the Touring Club de France, and therefore lays a more than common stress on the outdoor life.

Below, in the town, it is different. It could hardly be other than different, for this town shelters the shrine of Bernadette, and is arguably the last true centre of Christian pilgrimage left in the modern world. Here just over a hundred years ago, a strange event occurred.

In January 1858, a local girl, Bernadette Soubirous, had a vision. She was walking along the river west of the town and in a grotto in the rocks saw the apparition of the Virgin.

Over the next few weeks Bernadette, accompanied by a growing crowd of the curious, saw the Virgin no less than eighteen times, and in the course of one appearance was led to discover a spring, which was soon said to possess miraculous powers. People flocked there in their tens of thousands and have done so ever since.

From the pilgrims, those visions and that spring, all that you now see at Lourdes has developed. If you find much of it commercial or distressing, then spare a thought for the unhappy Bernadette. The Church completely took charge of her. She entered the religious life as a postulant at the Convent of St. Guildard at Nevers on the Loire in 1866 when she was twenty-two. Her treatment there was less than kind, and she died, a most unhappy woman, in 1879. If you visit St. Guildard today you can see the body of Bernadette, lightly coated with wax, displayed in a glass case, an object for the devout and the plain curious.

*　　*　　*

I had been told and advised to give Lourdes a miss; I wanted to, but travel writing has its duties, and so I went there and I am now glad that I did. Much of the place is every bit as spoilt and commercial as rumour says it is, so much so that it should be visited for that reason alone. This is the absolute end! When it comes to commercialised religion, and for the ultimate in *kitsch,* can you

*The Basilica, Lourdes*

beat *"a one-metre high, see-through, plastic replica of the Virgin, with an unscrewable gold crown which, once removed, enables you to fill the image with holy water from a tap"!* And yet, when you have descended the Boulevard de La Grotte — and I resist the pun — past all the models, the plaques, the tawdry junk and the plain rubbish, and enter the park of the Basilica, the place has something. The Basilica was built over the grotto in 1889, and is quite impressive, plated with votive panels, but it is the people who hold your attention.

Perhaps it is the children, either the healthy ones in great parties, with their smiling nuns. Perhaps it is the parents, ever hopeful, taking their children to the shrine, and maybe it is the smiles of the crippled children, whose courage puts you to shame. Whatever it is, you cannot laugh at them, and through all the money-grubbing the true Bernadette still shines. Millions of people have called on Ste

Bernadette, and somewhere, perhaps she listens. One sceptic among tens of thousands of believers feels very much alone.

In the end, if you stay a little while it all becomes very human. How else could so many get holy water but from a tap? And if the candles are sold from great racks, the money for them is taken on trust. No one asks for it and no one cheats. The grotto where Bernadette saw the Virgin lies past the basilica in the rocks by the river. Smoke-blackened now, it is hung with crutches, relics of miracles, and to the kneeling pilgrims a sign of hope. There is little charity, less faith, and hardly any hope in the world today, so I am glad I went to Lourdes, and suspect you might be too.

*　　*　　*

Tarbes is different yet again. It lies a little to the north of Lourdes, past the airport which ferries in the pilgrims to Lourdes and in the valley of the Adour, which we last met at Bayonne. Tarbes is a very old town and quite large. It suffered terribly during the Hundred Years War when the English held it from 1360 to 1406 and again during the Wars of Religion, being burnt three times between 1569 and 1595. It stands in lush farming country and is a noted centre for horse breeding, so that one place you ought to visit is the Musée Massey, which contains, of all things, a collection of Hussar uniforms, relics of the most dashing form of cavalry. Every county you can imagine is represented, and there are over a hundred gorgeous uniforms on display, a really dazzling collection of military splendour, with frogged tunic and *sabretasche*.

The *haras* or stud can also be visited and the animals, particularly the young foals are as always delightful, skipping about in the meadows, but never far from Mum.

The *Hotel Foch* is comfortable and recalls a local hero, for Tarbes was the birthplace of Marshal Foch, who commanded the Allied Armies in the closing stages of the Great War. The *Bigourdens* are naturally very proud of their great general, so much so that a house in Arreau, on the *pays de Neste,* which we will visit later, is marked with a plaque honouring the house as the birthplace of his *grandmother!*

We must get back to the mountains and the Lavedan, so let us go to Bagnères de Bigorre. This was the first town I ever visited in the Bigorre, and there at ten o'clock one morning I was introduced to the local specific, the *pousse rapière,* or 'sword thrust', which consists of champagne with a tot of Armagnac. Several thrusts of this finished me off for the day. The other memory of the time is of *garbure*, the local potato soup, which you can consume at every meal if you are not careful, and delicious though it is, you may find it rather filling.

Bagnères is of course a spa and like Tarbes stands on the Adour, but is most useful as a centre for excursions into the Baronnies, a truly Bigourden region which lies a little to the east and for which Bagnères is the market town. This is a region of remote hills, little farms, pasture land, still totally unspoilt, and rarely visited, although you should visit the abbey at Escale à Dieu. It is seamed with little roads and tracks and overlooked by the *Casque du Leris,* a sharp peak standing 1595m above the Campan valley.

If you make your way to Escots in the very heart of the Baronnies, you will be as far from the madding crowd as you can reasonably hope to be, and yet within a few miles of a main city.

We will look there and down the beautiful Campan valley, but we go west now, on a minor road, through Juncalalas, under the Pic du Jer, past the ski resort of Hautacam, and turn south for Luz-St-Saveur and Cauterets.

This is another *pays,* the *pays de Gave,* and we have a choice at Soulom, so let us first follow the *gave* de Cauterets up to the Pont d'Espagne.

*     *     *

Cauterets is a large attractive holiday town and owes much of its present success to the Franco-Prussion War. Before then, the *haute-monde* of Paris had gone into Germany to take the waters at Baden-Baden, or Marienbad, but consorting with the enemy was now unthinkable, and a new centre being needed, the fashionable chanced on Cauterets. It had in fact been a spa since medieval times, and the entire valley was ceded to the Benedictines of St. Savin in about 950 AD by County Raymond of Bigorre, who charged them to heal the sick by regular bathing in the thermal springs. They used to say *"A Cauterets tout que gareux"* — "At Cauterets all will be cured".

77

It is still a spa and still fashionable, although mostly as a ski resort. You can still swim in the warm mineral baths fed from underground springs. The wooden railway station dates from the turn of the century, and seen in the snow, is pure Tolstoy, while the cable car lurches over the rooftops off to the slopes on the Mont le Lys. The National Park of the Pyrénées begins just above Cauterets, and a museum and information centre in Cauterets will tell you all about the district. If you need a guide or a good meal you will find both at the *Hôtel Trois Pics* in the centre, before you press on up the road.

This is a spectacular route, for the valley is steep now. The waterfalls and torrents of the *gave* shoot past on every side, until the road levels out and ends at the bridge of Pont d'Espagne. From here you will have to walk and if you have the time you should certainly do so, for I know of nowhere in the Pyrénées more delightful, either for walking in summer or ski touring in winter. The whole area, but especially that to the west towards the Balaïtous, is a maze of paths, lakes and peaks, popular in summer but never overcrowded.

You can, if you wish, pick up the GR.10 here, and follow it east, down the valley of the Ossoue, to Gavarnie, and across into my favourite High Pyrenean region, the *pays Toy*. Who can resist going to Toyland?

*     *     *

Luz St. Saveur is the centre for the *pays Toy,* and has some special charms of its own. The village is dominated by a unique fortified church, and while many churches are fortified, this church is a fortress first complete with walls and battlements. It is attributed, incorrectly, to the Templars, but was actually crenellated by the Hospitalers at the end of the 14th century, probably after the English garrison of the castle of Ste. Marie on the next hill had had their throats cut.

The English came into Bigorre at the start of the Hundred Years War, and were only expelled in 1406. Napoleon III and Empress Eugenie came frequently to this region, and built the Pont Napoleon which leads up to the great *cirque* of Gavarnie. This is

*Church, Luz-St-Saveur*

*Cirque de Gavarnie*

one of the natural wonders of the region and the most famous natural attraction in the Pyrénées.

The *cirque* de Gavarnie is a great sheer wall, streaked with waterfalls, about 3000 metres high. It is reached on foot or mule, even on horseback, from the village of Gavarnie itself, and the trip from village to *cirque* takes about two hours.

You can take a path up the right hand side of the valley from the church at Gavarnie, and this gives good views of the *cirque* and the great waterfall that spins from the top on the trail to the Breche de Roland, that cleft in the *cirque* supposedly carved out by Roland before he fell at Roncesvalles. He must have had very long arms! There are two such passes, the *Breche,* and the *Fausse Breche* a few

80

*Brêche de Roland*

hundred metres further on, and if you walk up there you can stay in the C.A.F. hut below the summit before you return, perhaps crossing the frontier for a scramble on Mont Perdido (3355m). The *cirque de Gavarnie* is the one that gets all the attention but descending travellers should also visit the equally attractive cirque de Troumouse, along the *gave* de Héas above Luz.

*   *   *

There is superb walking all around Luz and Gavarnie and on the way into Gavarnie you will find by the roadside a statue of Count Henry Russell, a mountaineer and a noted eccentric. Russell was an Irishman by descent, but French by birth, being born in Toulouse. His title came from the 'Black Nobility' of the Vatican. He adored mountains and had climbed in the Himalayas and South America, before he came to the Pyrénées and found a region that fascinated and occupied him until his death in 1909. Russell climbed the Vignamale peak no less than thirty-three times, and made innumerable ascents elsewhere. I am not a climber but I am told that most of his 'climbs' were more like stiff walks or scrambles, but whatever their technical merit, he played a major part in opening up the Pyrénées to climbers without upsetting the sensibilities of the local people.

Later in life he tunnelled out cave homes in the mountains, where he would wine and dine his guests by candlelight in full evening dress, and at the age of seventy once spent seventeen days on the Vignamale, including yet another ascent to the summit.

Luz, which welcomes walkers in their hundreds every year, is full of good hotels and is the ideal place to stay in for Gavarnie, or the *pays Toy,* although those with a mind for tradition may prefer the *Hôtel des Voyageurs* at Gavarnie. Either centre will serve before you go east again to Barèges and over the col du Tourmalet.

*     *     *

This central region of the Lavedan is dominated by the great peak of the Pic du Midi de Bigorre (2865 metres) covered today with a radio and television antenna. South of this lies the lake region of the Néouvielle, which divides Luz from the valley of St. Lary.

The road up from Luz to Tourmalet is spectacular, and another route that any traveller should follow. Barèges, at the foot of the pass today shelters the unfortunates of the French Parachute Corps, those who fell upon stony ground, and those fitter ones being introduced to mountain warfare. For civilians it was and still is a famous spa.

Madam de Maintenon brought the young Duc de Maine here several times seeking a cure for his consumption and her letters to Louis XIV concerning the health of his favourite son were the first steps in a course that led to their eventual marriage.

It is now a ski centre, with a lift system linked with that of La Mongie across the Col du Tourmalet. The steep road between is a popular route for the Tour de France cycle race, poor devils! Tourmalet is the highest *col* in the Pyrénées, and late snow often sends the cyclists elsewhere.

*Count Henri Russel*

From Barèges the road winds on, steep and ever steeper, even more stark and beautiful, with the Pic du Midi shining above, until you cross the *col* and descend to La Mongie. Or you will if you are lucky.

On several visits I have found the *col* open only once, in August and even in mid-July snow can make this road impassable. The *col* stands at 2115 metres, the highest road in the French Pyrénées, and here, naturally enough, the snow comes early and stays late, so check if the path is clear before you cross.

You can walk from the Tourmalet north, to the Lac Bleu, high in the hills, around the Pène Blanque, and down to the valley of the Lesponne, or carry on through La Mongie to St. Marie de Campan. La Mongie is a modern ski resort encircled by a steep range of fearsome cliffs and rather prone to avalanches in winter. You will see that the road down to Ste. Marie is protected by avalanche shields and in winter anyway they are quite a comfort.

The valley of Campan, which runs up to Bagnères de Bigorre is pleasant and very green, watered by the Adour and bordered on the east by the Baronnies. Although marked by marble quarries, this valley is one of the most beautiful in the Hautes-Pyrénées, a carpet of wild flowers in the spring, green set against white peaks and a blue sky.

To the south the road runs to the lake at Payolle set among the woods and overlooked by the peak of the Arbizon (2831m). The *Hôtel Artouste* by the shore at Payolle is very good and therefore very popular, a great centre for cross country skiing in the winter. From Payolle it is on, up winding roads over the Col d'Aspin, and down to Arreau in the valley of the Aure.

Arreau is a pretty village and the birthplace of General Foch's grandmother, which should have you there in a trice, and stands at the point where the *Neste* de Luron rushes in to join the *Neste* de Aure, and this alone tells you we have left the *pays de gave* and are now in the *pays de Neste*.

\*     \*     \*

The *Hôstellerie de Val d'Aure* in Cadéac is a good place to stay, with proprietors who really know the mountains and the sites to see round about, notably the Romanesque door of the church of St.

*Country near Barèges*

Exupery. We have managed to keep away from churches for a while so you should see this one. The road south from Cadéac leads to St. Lary Soulan, another ski centre, with most of the slopes set on the Pla d'Adet above the town, but this road leads on, and eventually through a tunnel into Spain, one of the few direct routes through these mountains across the divide.

We, however, intend to stay on this side of the frontier and can turn off by Fabien and head into the really remote region, the massif du Néouvielle. Bigorre is a marvellous region for the walker. The mountains are spectacular and the many lakes make perfect objects for a days ramble, enough to keep you there for weeks.

Finally though, we must press on, east to the blue sea, so it is back to Arreau to follow the *Neste du Louron* up to the little chapel of St. Pé de la Moraine, over the Col de Peyresourde (2000m) and, by crossing that ridge, leave the beautiful Bigorre behind and descend into the *comté* of Comminges.

# 5 · Comminges
# and the Couserans

When we reach Comminges we are half way across the Pyrénées, and at the point of change. Here the Val d'Aran juts up into France, and so divides the two separate arms of the Pyrénées which, as we saw before, do not run directly across the neck of land between the two countries in a straight line. The range is split by this geological fault, through which the Garonne (or Garona) flows over into France.

The Romans laid the foundations of the Comminges we see today, when Pompey the Great came up from Iberia and founded, among other centres, the settlement of *Lugdunum Convenarum*, which in the Christian era became Bertrand de Comminges. The country has been over-run by the Vandals and was part of the County of Toulouse until the Albigensian Crusade. It was then occupied by the English who were only driven out in 1453, the year of Castillion.

Comminges has always been linked to the Couserans on the east, and consists of a series of valleys running out south and east from St. Lizier. The Couserans, like the Barronies of Bigorre, are an undiscovered country full of little by-ways and the perfect place to wander off the beaten track.

When you wind down from the *col* de Peyresourde, although out of Bigorre, you are still in the *pays de Neste*. Coming in from the south is the Neste d'Oo, a torrent fed by the beautiful Lac de Oo up on the frontier. If you wished you could follow this *neste* on foot from Luchon up to the lake and then follow the GR.10 which passes this way up to the heights of Superbagnères, the ski-centre overlooking the Valley of Luchon. Before you do so though, stop in St. Aventin and inspect the church. Guide books often labour over churches, but this one is a pearl of the Romanesque.

The heights of Superbagnères are open and windswept, crowned with a massive but elegant Edwardian hotel and much beloved today by the hang-gliding fraternity who were launching themselves off down the ski runs, and circling away across the depths to the valley below. You get superb views from here, west across to the mountains of Ariège and south to the Maladeta massif, which lies in Spain and contains, in the Pic d'Aneto (3404m) the highest peak of the entire range.

Passing down near the waterfall, the Cascade d'Enfer, you descend the valley of the Lip and so arrive in elegant Luchon, the

*Luchon*

*Hang-gliding, Superbagnères*

archetypal Pyrénean spa, and now a bustling resort in summer and winter. This is the place for skiers, for walkers, for all lovers of the *haute montagne* and the not-too-terribly-ill.

Known today as Bagnères de Luchon it was once the Roman spa of *Thermes Onesiens,* a shrine of the god Ilixo. Luchon was a popular resort as far back as the first century A.D., and has been greeting visitors ever since. It is very elegant, calm, a place of repose, but you will eat well at the *"La Rotonde,"* which serves regional dishes.

There are many Roman remains in and around Luchon, although the Roman city was devastated by the invading Burgundians when the Empire crumbled in about 450 A.D. Many of the ruins have only been excavated recently and are therefore in excellent condition.

During the Middle Ages, the valley passed through everyone's hands, belonging to the French, English or Aragonese in turn as well as to whatever local war-lord gained temporary control. The old town was finally ruined by a fire in 1723, which only the church survived, and the town you see today dates, with much building and rebuilding, from about 1750.

The first modern thermal baths were set up in 1815, and the town became instantly popular with veterans of the Napoleonic Wars. The springs which feed the thermal baths are all notably radio-active, a grisly thought, but the waters are said to be efficacious in treating ailments of the throat and lungs. Personally, I put my faith in wine and good food, and for both would recommend a visit to the little Logis the *Hôtel Bon Accueil* in the Place Joffre.

For lovers of the outdoors, Luchon has a lot to offer and the Syndicate d'Initiative has a large collection of maps and guides available, illustrating the many local walks and rides. As a glance at the map will tell you, Luchon lies south and west of the frontier, which here thrusts north along the Val d'Aran up to the Pic de Buchanère (2193m). South of the town up the Valley of the Pique lies the great pass of Venasque, a famous route into the Hautes-Pyrénées, leading directly over to the Maladeta range which is dominated by the Pic d'Aneto, at 3404m. the highest point in the Pyrénées. Luchon is surrounded by mountains and spectacular roads, but none so startling as that to the Port de Venasque past the Hospice de France. This is a wild spot, but one you cannot really miss. Here is the real Pyrénées, dark, brooding and beautiful, loud with water, veiled by clouds and rain.

Although there is a road, you cannot at present drive up to the Hospice. The banks have been eroded and earth and trees now block the route in several places, and anyway this is a place to approach on foot. You can drive up from Luchon, but before long you will have to leave the road for a while and take to the footpaths under the cliffs of the gorge of the River Pique, before you can regain the road, now falling into ruin, below the Hospice itself.

When you arrive at the Hospice you will usually find the grass outside dotted with small tents, and littered with resting walkers. A stream flows down from Venasque, and sheep-bells tinkle. From

*Towards the Port de Venasque*

the Hospice parties leave for the Port de Venasque, and the Val d'Aran, and the site of the Hospice, surrounded as it is by crags and dark cliffs, is really magnificent. Until 1978 the Hospice, which is now a ramshackle collection of buildings occupied by herdsmen and shepherds during the *transhumance,* was a successful inn, owned by one Odon Harrillion, a high mountain guide and a real character.

There are still guides available in the Pyrénées but their heyday was back in the '20s and '30s when people, or at any rate wealthy people, could take long holidays, and the mountains were a fashionable place for English milords with time to spare.

It was then the custom for people on holiday to walk the Pyrénées from east to west. Their guides would collect them at Perpignan, complete with mules, tents and stores, rather like an African safari, and lead the party west. There were no C.A.F. huts in those days and the mountain inns were as Belloc reminds us, full of those:

> *Fleas that tease*
> *In the High Pyrénées*

After the Second World War the Hospice de France became famous for its food and *ambiance,* not with the Smart Set but with those who liked the mountains and prefer solitary travel on foot or skis. This little inn was the place where the trails met. I remember a brief visit there in the late 1950s, when I spoke little French and so spent the evening silent by the fire, drinking wine and gazing at the people who kept coming in out of the howling night. Wet dogs steamed before the open fire and the wine and talk flowed around the tables. The scene was medieval, as indeed was the Hospice itself. The building dates from the 11th century and must have seen all kinds of people, from the Santiago pilgrims to Belloc's *"Modern Traveller"* over the centuries, but the great days of the Hospice are all over now. It is always a mistake to go back to the keener memories of your youth. Everything looks smaller and shabbier. The Hospice is shut and shuttered now and falling into ruin, but the hills are still there and the people still trudge past. Perhaps someone will come along and open it again. I hope so anyway.

\*   \*   \*

Well now, why be gloomy? This is a beautiful spot and from your tent by the Hospice you have a choice of routes and fine walks in all directions. The classic trail is over into Spain, by the Port de Venasque into the Maladeta range which lies to the South. The frontier runs north here, the mountains following the Garona up to the town of St. Beat, which was hurriedly fortified to block this invasion route.

The Val d'Aran came to be Spanish almost by accident. It was the route through which troops were fed into France for the Flanders campaigns of the 16th century, and as such it became a debating point at the making of the Treaty of the Pyrénées. The Spanish negotiators remarked at the conference that *"of course the Val d'Aran would be Spanish"* and, as the maps were inaccurate, and the French wished the frontier to stand on the watershed they agreed, not realising that the valley was a highway into France, and that although the Luchon *cirques* are higher the true watershed lies to the South. The chief town of the Val d'Aran is Viella, and nearby lies the *exact* centre of the Pyrénean chain at the *col* de Bonaigua, where the Garonne rises, and as the Garona, starts its journey north to the Atlantic.

This *col* is the true watershed between France and Spain, and ought to mark the frontier, but this point was overlooked during the negotiations of 1659 and so the Val d'Aran remains Spanish as far north as Pont du Roi, ten miles below St. Beat and some twenty miles north of the direct east-west line of the frontier at the Port de Venasque.

St. Beat is called the *cle de France,* the key in the lock guarding Comminges and France itself from invasion. This is the home town of Marshal Gallieni, who has some claims to being the true hero of the Battle of the Marne, in 1914, and is yet another example of how many famous Great War Generals came from the Pyrénées. Foch came from Tarbes in Béarn, and Joffre from Rivesaltes in the Corbières.

St. Beat is a fortified town with the keep of a 14th century castle, and stands on the now French Garonne, which is fed from now on by every torrent as it heads north for Toulouse, past the great site of Comminges, the church and monastery of St. Bertrand.

\*     \*     \*

St. Bertrand-de-Comminges is spectacular. The great building stands up on a long hill overlooking the countryside for miles around, and as a great ship rides the waves, soars above the surrounding plain. Like Luchon, this was a Roman settlement and a spa. The site was first occupied by Iberian tribesmen driven from Spain by the Romans, but Pompey overwhelmed their newly established settlement and established instead of the town of *Lugdunum Convenarum* here in 72 B.C., as a rest centre for his legions. It became a noted spa and was a favourite place of exile for those banished from Rome. Herod Antipas, the Tetrach of Galilee, withdrew here hastily in 37 A.D. after incurring the wrath of Caligula, and many other noble Romans followed in his path until their villas and baths were destroyed by Burgundian invaders in 408 A.D. The ruins of their city lie in the plain below the monastery.

The hilltop remained a jumble of ruined stone until the early 12th century when Bertrand de l'Isle Jourdain, Bishop of Comminges, decided that this would be the perfect site for his cathedral, not least because Comminges was and is a region famous for its marble.

The cathedral is partly Romansque, partly Gothic, and partly Rennaissance. With the increasing number of Compostella pilgrims who passed this way coming from the east, the original church soon became too small, and it was enlarged in the 14th century by the orders of another Bertrand, Bertrand de Got, who later ruled at Avignon as Pope Clement V. The cathedral structure was finished in 1352, and as you will see it is a vast building, with an exquisite cloister and magnificent choir screen and stalls, dating from 1535, which will repay inspection.

St. Bertrand de Comminges himself, the founder of the cathedral, is also buried here and he has a secular memorial in the Gallery of Trophies, a collection of Roman carvings and statues, which he himself began. The collection dates from the 1st century A.D. and was discovered during the building operations.

The choir is a fine example of Rennaissance art. The carving is full of religious and secular imagery, and the *miséricordes* are quite amusing with carvings of monks fighting for their seats or being scourged, or simply falling down and resting.

St. Bertrand today is a small place, with barely 300 inhabitants, submerged by tourists, but you will eat well at the *Du Comminges*

94

*Cathedral of St Bertrand*

and this too is a place you cannot miss. This is a feature of the Pyrénées. The mountains are entirely delightful but here and there, as at Comminges, is a place which is quite unique, and which no traveller can afford to pass by.

Not far away, across the valley floor, is another fine Romansque church, the basilica of St. Just at Valcabrère. This was built to commemorate two early Church martyrs, St. Just and St. Pastor, executed hereabouts by Diocletian. This was the cathedral before St. Bertrand's was built on the nearby hill and dates from the time of Charlemagne.

Surrounded by dark cypress trees and set in green fields, St. Just is a beautiful church and like so many Romanesque buildings, full of exquisite carvings. So stop here too for a while, before turning north.

*　　*　　*

We are following the Garonne now, so for a while let us go north, visiting the Black Virgin in the Chapel of Poligan, then through Montrejeu and then east to St. Gaudens, sometime home of the Bishops of Comminges and now, inevitably, a tourist centre. It contains an interesting museum, and a few good hotels, notably *l'Esplanade*, but need not detail us long, for it is better to press on to the Valley of the Salat and the towns of St. Lizier and St. Girons.

St. Girons is unremarkable but St. Lizier is a little gem. Stay in the *Hôtel de la Tour* and look about you. St. Lizier stands at the tip of the Couserans, on a hill overlooking the Salat, and the trout from this river are the speciality of the town. The cathedral of St. Lizier is a riot of Romanesque, with carved capitals in the cloister where Simon de Montfort signed the agreement as leader of the Albigensian Crusade, an event which spelt out the ruin of the House of Toulouse, and lead Simon to his death.

St. Lizier is the place to stay for forays south into the Couserans, reached from the west by yet another col, the *col* de Portet d'Aspet.

*　　*　　*

Every traveller likes to find an unexpected area. To find somewhere undiscovered, even in the common use of the term, is

*Cloisters, St Bertrand's*

now rather difficult, but there are plenty of places less well known than they might be, and with a good deal to offer to the stranger. Just such a place is the Couserans, which lies like an open fan below St. Lizier.

It is a green, rolling country, a 'land of eighteen valleys' broken and fairly high, running up on the frontier to over 2000 metres. Coming over the *col* d'Aspet you have a clear run down through St. Lary to Castillon, chief town and centre for the Valley of Bethmale, with its beautiful bell tower on the chapel of St. Pierre. You can follow the valley down through the village of Bethmale and then up to the open *col* de la Core, where the GR.10 reappears out of the mist. Do not rush across this country. Turn off to Portet, or walk south to Mont Vallier (2838m) named after St. Vallier, Bishop of the Couserans, before you descend to the village of Seix.

This is again in the Valley of the Haut-Salat and magnificent country. The river runs north through Seix out of the mountains to the south. Seix is, in fact, a better centre for the valleys than St. Lizier, for they run off in every direction from here and the countryside is both rugged and beautiful. So stay in Seix at the *Auberge des Deux Rivières,* before it is time to go east again. You are already in Ariège.

*     *     *

We must go east to Foix, along the road from St. Girons, but on the way let us stop at Lescure and go north to see the great grotto at the Mas d'Azil. This is a huge cave hollowed out in the escarpment of Plantural by the river Arize. The road follows the river through the mountain, which opens like a great moth to swallow you up.

Once under the hill we turn east under the ridge and run down to Foix, capital of the Counts, and centre for the green Cathar country of Ariège.

# 6 · Ariège

The Ariège is a large region, straddling the Pyrénées from Comminges in the west, south to Andorra, and west to the edge of Roussillon. It includes the comté of Foix, and the *pays* of Leze, Olmes and Foix, as well as 'High' and 'Low' Ariege and, today at least, the Couserans, which for historic reasons we have attached to the previous chapter.

In many ways the Ariège is a microcosm of all the Pyrénées, for it combines within its boundaries some elements of all the features found elsewhere, besides, and this too is typical of the Pyrénées, having some unique features of its own. Ariège is in many ways wilder than Bigorre, and her hills are harder to get into, and steeper to climb.

From the Mas d'Azil it is an easy run across the *pays de Foix*, and through green countryside under the crest of the Montagnes du Plantaurel to the city of Foix. This fine town stands on the River Ariège, which here, as in most French regions gives its name to the département.

Ariège is probably my favourite region in the whole Pyrénées, mainly because it is full of little hidden valleys with those castles and towers which I happen to like very much, and a land of soldiers. *"Ariège produces men of iron"* said Napoleon.

This is the ancestral home of the Counts of Foix, of whom Gaston Phoebus is only one illustrous example. The Counts seem to have had more than their share of common sense and as this is unusual in any age, they managed particularly well in the Middle Ages and extended their inheritance generation after generation. They controlled the great fortress of Carcassonne, shared the lordships of Andorra with the Bishop of Urgel, married into the family of Navarre and served the French crown for centuries as generals and constables of armies, all from their power-base in Foix, which they took care to guard tenaciously. Apart from feudal dues and road tolls, the Counts gained much of their wealth from mining iron ore in the Vicdessos Valley near Niaux, a seam so rich it was only worked out in 1931 leaving a valley under the *pic* de la Madelon which is remote and very beautiful.

Foix is an exciting town to visit, with remnants of the walls, and overshadowed by the great castle. There has been a castle here for nearly a thousand years. The first Count of Foix, Roger-Bernard, came to live here in 1002 A.D. It resisted the Albigensian crusaders under Simon de Montfort, but fell to Philip the Bold in 1272, and was practically abandoned when the Counts gained the lordship of Béarn in 1290 with the marriage of Roger-Bernard III to Margarite de Béarn. It remained a garrison, under the command of a seneschal. Gaston Phoebus chose Orthez as his capital, since this was already the capital of Béarn. The castle now contains a museum, like so many of the old buildings, and this one is devoted to the history and pre-history of Ariège, although you can also pant your way up to the top of the central keep, and gain great views over the town and valley.

Foix *ville* is worth exploring, with pleasant hotels like the Logis *Audoye Lons,* and at least one excellent restaurant called, inevitably, the *Phoebus*, and the interesting *Maison des Cariatides* in the centre. You can also enjoy traditional cuisine at *La Bartacane,* in the Avenue de Lérida.

Apart from the medieval sights Foix contains one natural marvel, the underground river of Labouiche. You can run through this subterranean torrent by boat, a trip of over three kilometres, passing curious rock formations and waterfalls on every side, and there are fine views of the Château at Foix from the embarkation point.

Foix is an excellent centre for visiting Ariège, and most of the surrounding *pays* are within easy reach with a choice of route in every direction.

North lies Pamiers, in Basse-Ariège, skirting the plain of Toulouse. Pamiers is quite a large town, medieval of course, with canals, crenellated walls, and tall bell towers in the style *Tolousain*. Gabriel Faure was born here in 1845, and the town has strong artistic and cultural traditions.

Pamiers was staunchly orthodox during the Albigensian Crusade of the 13th century, and became a bishopric in 1295. The town has several large churches in consequence, notably Notre Dame du Camp, and the cathedral of Mercadel. It also has many good hotels, the *Hôtel de France* being a good place to stay and *Restaurant Vitract* or the *Le Parc* are good places to eat.

Ariège was savaged in the Albigensian Crusade and if you travel east from Pamiers, you enter the Cathar country at Mirepoix, one of the centres of that tormented religion. Mirepoix was a *bastide*,

*The hill of Montségur*

erected after the Albigensian Crusade, and seat of the Mirepoix-Levis family, supporters of Simon de Montfort. You may be tempted to skirt Mirepoix, for it is only a little place but if you press on into the centre you will find it fascinating. Like all the best *bastides* it has a central square, with arched houses overhanging the pavement, narrow alleys running off in all directions and a fortified church, which was elevated to a cathedral in 1506. This is our first town in the *payes Cathare* and since we are going to hear a lot about them from now on, we should discuss them here.

*   *   *

The Cathars were a heretical sect, which preached a gospel of extreme purity, maintaining among other things, that man himself was inherently vile, and since God was perfect, man was a creation of the Devil. To put it simply, the Cathars were dualists. Dualism existed within the body of the Christian Church from quite early days, and the elements of the dualist creed were expounded by Marcion in Rome in about 144 A.D. The essence of dualism is this: God is good and all-powerful, and yet evil exists in the world and can be seen to flourish. Therefore God could not be the creator of the world, which clearly was the work of the Devil. There were therefore two 'Gods' — one of good, one of evil. So, taking this a stage further, if Man was to reach Heaven, he must separate himself from the world, denying himself all worldly pleasures and practising self-denial to a point which, for most people, was impossible.

The Cathar Church, which sprung from this dogma, fell into two broad classifications. The word *Cathar* comes from the Greek and means purified, and those who accepted the rigours of the Cathar faith received the baptism or *consolamentum* and became *Perfecti*. They swore to forego all luxuries, to travel only with other *Perfecti*, to deny themselves marriage and the pleasures of the flesh. However, many believing Cathars found it impossible to live like this, and although followers of the sect, abstained from the *consolamentum* until just before their death.

By the middle of the 12th century the Cathar Church was large and well organized. It was deeply rooted in the provinces of Languedoc and supported by the Counts of Toulouse, and many knights and nobles. All this was deeply worrying to the Catholic Church and in particular to the Pope.

The piety of the *Perfecti* and the example of their lives made the wealth and luxury of Church prelates look remarkably sinful. The tenants of the Cathar faith seemed to exercise a wide appeal, and anyway much of it was fundamentally heretical since it denied the possibility of repentance and divine forgiveness. This alone was enough to get the supporters of such a doctrine condemned to the stake, but apart from their religious appeal, the Cathars were a political force and this, as we shall see, eventually led to their extirpation.

Mirepoix, our first stop, was a Cathar stronghold, held for the Count of Toulouse and destroyed in the Crusade. It was then rebuilt by the Levis family, who were supporters of Simon de Montfort, leader of the Crusade. He appointed Guy de Levis Marshal of Foix and charged him with suppressing Catharism in the district. The town was reconstructed as a *bastide* in about 1279, and still contains many typical bastide features, although the church was not completed until the last century, after taking four hundred years to erect.

*     *     *

South of Mirepoix we enter the *pays de Olmes* and come to Lavelanet. You can reach this town easily by the minor road which leaves Mirepoix to the east through Lagarde with another *château fort* and Chalabre and so to Puivert, which lies just outside Ariège, in the Aude. This castle at Puivert is another Cathar stronghold, which fell to the Crusaders in 1210. The castle can and should be visited and there you can inspect the carvings of troubadours inside the central tower. The Languedoc was the true home of the troubadours, but their art, like the Cathars, vanished in the Crusade.

Belesta, on the road to Lavelanet is a pretty place, a good walking centre, and you should visit the Chapel of the Val d'Amour above the little river, a delightful spot.

Lavelanet is the capital of the *pay d'Olmes,* and a textile centre. The town is unremarkable, but the countryside round about is splendid, and from here you can visit the last Cathar stronghold at

Montsegur, a little way to the South, the final and decisive battleground of the Albigensian Crusade.

The Albigensian Crusade, which flayed Southern France between 1208 and 1229, was a curious event. Although the word had less meaning then it was a crusade of "Frenchmen" against "Frenchmen". If the origins were religious the mainspring was political and the motivation greed.

Innocent III launched the crusade after a papal legate had been murdered by a knight in the service of Raymond of St. Gilles, Count of Toulouse. The Pope claimed also that Raymond sheltered the heretical Cathars, or was one himself. Phillip Augustus, King of France, was reluctant to war with Raymond since he was busy at the time driving King John of England from his lands in Normandy, but the French clergy preached the Crusade, and since the South, the land of the *langue d'Oc*, was well known to be rich, soft and ready for plunder, Northern knights flocked to take the cross.

The Crusade began with the fall of Béziers in 1209 and the massacre of the population. From that point on blood flowed like wine. Cathars were captured and burned in vast holocausts after every capitulation. Cities were taken, sacked, re-taken, and sacked again. As the anarchy spread, outside forces moved in. Pedro II of Aragon took the field on the part of Toulouse, claiming that the Crusaders were warring on his vassals, not for the Pope and religion but for the King of France and personal profit.

Late in 1209, the Crusaders, who needed a general, elected as their leader a knight of the Ile de France, one Simon de Montfort, father of that other Simon de Montfort who, as Earl of Leicester, established the English Parliament.

Simon defeated and killed Pedro of Aragon at Murat in 1213, but was killed besieging Toulouse in 1218. His son took up the struggle and, although the Count of Toulouse eventually defeated the Crusaders, the terms agreed for his reconcilation with the Church were to lead to the extinction of their house. By 1229 the Crusade was over, but Cathar strongholds remained, and the Inquisition began to eliminate them one by one. Over three hundred heretics were burned in one day at Moissac. In 1231, two years after the peace, nineteen were executed at an *auto-de-fé* in Toulouse.

Over six hundred villages in the Toulousain alone saw the

*The walls of Montségur*

Inquisition burn their neighbours before all eyes turned to the great Cathar fortress at Montségur.

\* \* \*

By the year 1240, the Albigensian Crusade was into the second generation. De Montfort was dead, much of the country devastated, and the House of Toulouse, although still in being, was worn out with the struggle. The *perfecti*, however, fought on and the lynch pin of their defence was the castle at Montségur. Even at first sight you will see why they were able to resist there for so long, for the site itself is formidable. Montségur stands on a high hill, 1000 metres above the valley, and even today you will find it a stiff climb up the rock-strewn slopes, without the problems of arrows or boiling oil. In 1243 the garrison of Carcassonne marched against the Cathars of Montségur, and began a siege that was to last nine months.

Assault on the walls proved difficult. The besiegers tried to starve the defenders out, but even this proved beyond the capabilities of the Crusaders. Support in the shape of food and fighting men, was entering the castle up to the end. Eventually a small party of Basques established themselves on the edge of the plateau and captured the eastern wall. With the possibility of assault now upon them, the Cathars offered to surrender and under the circumstances they were granted generous terms. All those who renounced Catharism and returned to the Church would be allowed to go free without further punishment, although, inevitably, the fire awaited the rest. The defenders were allowed two weeks to debate the matter and many Cathars took the *consulamentum* at this time. Finally, the gates were opened and those who refused to abjure were taken in chains to the field below the castle, and burned alive. Over two hundred knights and their families perished in this holocaust, and the place is still called The Field of Burning. Meanwhile, within the castle a mystery was developing which has endured to the present day.

When the Crusaders entered the castle, they met one serious disappointment. The fabled treasure of the Cathars, *"gold, silver and a great quantity of money"* which the castle was said to contain, has disappeared. Where it went to is a mystery, for it has

*Cathar Memorial below Montségur*

not been found to this day, but we will discuss it again later, at Rennes le Château.

This was not the last outpost of the Cathars. Quéribus in the Corbières did not fall until 1255, but the fall of Montségur finished the Cathars as a Church, and although you will see the Cathar cross on the wayside, the people and their faith have perished.

\* \* \*

Montségur is a necessary visit, and although Michelin says it will take nearly two hours to climb up there you can do it in less with considerable extra effort.

The climb is both steep and rocky. Your path must either be forced through bushes, or made by skirting unnerving drops, but the view from the top is worth it. The castle occupies most of the ridge and can only be explored by clambering up ladders or over piles of tumbled stones, to gain entrance to the interior. The roof of the castle has gone, but an open staircase leads you up to the walls, with dizzy views over the red roofs of Montsegur village far below and along the valley of the Lasset, through the gorges towards Belesta.

From Montségur, you the choice of several interesting excursions to make. A forest road from near Montferrier will take you most of the way to the top of the Mont d'Olmes and if you then gain the Pic de Han (2074m) you can make your way along the crest of the Montagne de Tabe to the Pic de St. Barthélemy (2348m), then north, down past the lakes, to join the footpath which will lead you back to Montségur.

*    *    *

South of Montségur, through the gorges of the Frau, skirting the very frontier of Ariège, you reach open farming country, on the edge of the Pays de Sault, and come to Montaillou.

This little village, overlooked by the remains of its ruined castle on a motte, has become famous in recent years following the publication of a scholarly work *'Montaillou, a Cathar Village'* by Leroy Ladurie (Scholar Press 1978). M. Leroy Ladurie described the history of this typical Ariège village during the Cathar period, and from his investigations has written the history of their lives, their marriages, liaisons and their eventual fate. The common people of the Middle Ages are the great unknown area for the historians, but these people drew themselves into the archives because of their devotion to a heretical religion, and so eventually into the history books.

Montaillou is a very ordinary village, but if you have read the history of its former inhabitants, who lived in these very houses, much altered now perhaps, but basically the same stones, you will find it difficult to look on any little village as just another place.

*    *    *

*Leper pool, Ax-les-Thermes*

South of Foix lies Tarascon-sur-Ariège, another old town, and a good centre for trips up into the Pyrénean range to the south. This is about as far as the region goes towards an industrial centre, for aluminium is smelted here, and the last iron furnace closed down only in the thirties.

The Cathars have their memorials here as well, for six hundred unrepentant heretics were walled up in the caves at Lombrive nearby, and starved to death.

People come here now for the excursions to visit the cave painting of prehistoric man at nearby Niaux, or to inspect the Cathar carvings at Ussat, which are said to provide clues to the location of the missing Cathar treasure. Similar symbols in the Grotto of Lombrive or the church at nearby Ornolac, arouse a considerable amount of interest, and are closely inspected by hopeful treasure hunters.

Passing down towards Ax you will see on your left the great but now ruined chateau of Urs, and pass through Luzenac, which all mothers ought to admire, as this is the world's great centre for the manufacture of baby powder. And so to Ax ...

*　　*　　*

Ax les Thermes is a spa and has been one for centuries. The Romans used the hot springs here, and St. Louis excavated the open bath, the *basin des Ladres* in the centre of the town for those of his soldiers who returned from the Seventh Crusade infected with leprosy. This steaming fountain, smelling of bad eggs, is usually surrounded by paddlers enjoying the 79°C temperature of the water.

Since these unhappy days, and while retaining its customers in search of the waters, Ax has become a ski centre and, in summer anyway, a mecca for walkers. The skiing takes place at Ax-1400 on the plateau of Bonascre, south of the town, while the local Syndicate has waymarked dozens of walks in the hills round about.

Ax lies below the plateau of the *pays de Sault*, which are reached over the col de Pradel, a point which gives views, on a good day, as far as the distant Corbières.

The gorges of Rebenty in the pays de Sault are another of those little out-of-the-way beauty spots which never get the attention they deserve, and from Ax anyway, most of the traffic flows south to Puymorens, to Andorra, and the high Cerdagne.

# 7 · Andorra and the Cerdagne

All Andora, and much of the Cerdagne, is a political and historic anachronism. Since they lie side by side in the Eastern Pyrénées we may consider them together, for they have much in common. All the people we will meet from now on, the inhabitants of Andorra, the Cerdagne and Roussillon are Catalans.

You can enter Andorra from France or Spain, on a wide modern road which spans this little country and is much favoured by large *camions,* either bringing in more supplies of duty-free goods for the bulging tourist traps or passing through Andorra simply to tank up with duty-free fuel.

That, stated simply, is the chief current attraction of this little state. Taxes are minimal. Expensive items ranging from cameras and radios to cigarettes and Scotch are duty-free and relatively cheap. It seems to be an effective inducement for the tourists swarm into Andorra in the summer, and you can have a long wait on the hill below the customs post at the Pas de la Case, where Andorran police in their plum-coloured uniforms watch the arrival of fresh customers with unconcealed relish.

That noted, Andorra has a long history and a certain curious charm. The main street of the capital, Andorra-La-Vella, could give greed, envy and avarice a bad name, but if you probe up the side streets and travel into the valleys you may find that Andorra has more to offer than discount.

Andorra is very mountainous and extremely small. A mere 500 square kilometres of hill and valley, which I convert to about 180 square miles. It is governed by a Council of State, elected locally from the six parishes, has no army, no currency, a minute police force and, apart from tourism, no external trade.

It is 'ruled' or co-owned in a feudal fashion by the Bishop of Urgel, representing the *cortes* of Spain, and the Prefect of Ariège, who has inherited the mantle of the Counts of Foix, and now represents the President of France. The full title is *'The Co-Principality of the Valleys of Andorra.'* Andorra pays an annual tribute of 450 pesetas to Spain and 960 francs to France, but both sums are now graciously remitted. The Andorrans will tell you that their little state was founded by Louis the Debonair, son of Charlemagne, but that's unlikely.

History does not tell us why Roger-Bernard III of Foix signed a treaty as co-suzerian with the Bishop of Urgel, still less why it has endured unbroken since 1278. Normally one side or the other would have seized the whole valley the minute he had the power to do so, and over the centuries there have been opportunities enough, but Andorra endures.

There are now about twenty-five thousand inhabitants, many there to avoid taxation in their homelands. The State is divided into six parishes each of which elects Councillors to serve in the *'Conseil de Terre'* which administers the principality. In spite of a charter attributed to Charlemagne, the constitution of Andorra was medieval, relying entirely on custom and usage, until 1789 when their laws were written down to prevent annexation by Spain, then at war with Revolutionary France. This written constitution was then placed in a chest with six locks, the keys being shared among the six parish councillors, so that no amendments or alterations could be carried out on the sly. The language of the people is Catalan, and indeed Andorra is the only place in the world where Catalan is the official language. When the road signs north point to *França,* you realise that the struggle to preserve an identity is always made up of little things.

*       *       *

The main town, some twenty miles south of the French frontier at Envalira, is Andorre-la-Vella, which contains about half the population and is the centre for commerce. The *Conseil de Terre* sits in the Maison des Vallées, and there you can inspect the ancient chest with its six locks, where the constitution and Charlemagne's charter is still secured. Andorra-la-Vella is the centre for the local tobacco industry, the growing — not the smuggling — and for the issue of postage stamps.

The countryside of Andorra is wild and very beautiful, with splendid views over the surrounding peaks. Andorra is trying to diversify its sources of revenue and so there is skiing now at Soldeu and the Pas de la Case, near Envalira which, incidentally, marks once again the divide between the Atlantic slopes of the Pyrénées and those of the Mediterranean, towards which we are now beginning to descend.

The road from Envalira to la Vella is very scenic, and if you stay in any of the small villages which line the route you will be better served than in the main township, for Andorran hospitality is famous, and the food reminiscent of Spain.

North of la Vella a minor road leads up through the Valera del Nord towards the frontier, but it peters out near the village of El Serrat, although you can cross the frontier on foot through the Port de la Rat. This is a wild region and should only be visited in summer.

The gorge of San Antoni is traversed by an old mule train path, and this is not so old either, for mules are still used for transport in the hills. This track leads up to La Massena, a centre for iron working. This valley was locally famous for its blacksmiths, and so at Ordino you can see the home of the former iron master who dug out the ore, Don Guillem, a Spanish title to a Catalan name. Above Ordino at La Cortinada, they grow tobacco, and even export it, which is curious because the smuggling of cigarettes from Andorra into Spain and France, where their sale is a State monopoly, is still an important Andorran occupation.

Unless you wish to explore it on foot, Andorra need not detain you long, but the hinterland has its attractions. Thanks to the magnet of duty-free shipping at La Vella, which consumes a lot of people's time, and more of their money, you will find the hills of Andorra quite deserted, so you could go there and never be

*Walkers below Mount Carlit*

disturbed. We must get on however, down again to L'Hospitalet and then up to the Col de Puymorens and up through Porté to my favourite place in Roussillon, the mountain plateau of the Cerdagne.

*   *   *

It is a good idea to come into the Cerdagne from the west through Porté. Coming the other way, up from the Aude valley or from Perpignan, the valley is enclosed and the true dimensions of the Cerdagne are not immediately obvious. Coming up from the west it appears as suddenly as a blow, a wide plateau stretching into the distance, surrounded by snow-tipped mountains, green, placid, bathed in warm sunlight, different, and very, very beautiful.

The Cerdagne is a country of constrasts. It slopes up to the north from the frontier of Spain, and has been a march since the 9th

114

century when Roussillon and Spanish Catalonia were recaptured from the Arabs by the Kings of Aragon.

The Cerdagne is a wide, fertile mountain valley, 3000 metres above the coastal plains. It supported a Marcher Lord, and, in 878 A.D. one of them, Wilfred, became Count of Barcelona and vassal to Aragon.

Over the next two hundred years, the Counts of Barcelona became great princes, virtually independent of their overlord, and by 1117 they controlled a whole coastal region of the Mediterranean from Barcelona to Perpignan, and inland as far as the territory of Toulouse. Much of this territory lies outside the Pyrénées, on the plains below, and so the lords of the Cerdagne ceased to be Marcher lords, spending their lives in armour, and the plateau itself became a peaceful country well inside the frontiers. Castles were unnecessary as the mountains gave protection enough, and farming flourished.

After the collapse of the Kingdom of Majorca in the 14th century the Cerdagne passed firmly into the hands of Aragon, and their kings held it until the *'reyes Catolicos'* united the Spanish Kingdoms in the late 15th century. It remained entirely Spanish until the Treaty of the Pyrénées in 1659, which established the Franco-Spanish frontier on the watershed of the Pyrénées. Or at least it tried to.

As we have seen with the Val d'Aran, the Treaty threw up many anomalies, mainly because each side sought to retain the advantage of defensible ground.

The top of the mountains would be the most natural frontier, and in the Cerdagne this would have led the boundary from Mont Carlit (2921m) across the Col del Pam (2005m) and the watershed at the Col de la Perche (1579m), then up to the peak at Cambras (2747m), and so across to Puigmal (2910m), on the present frontier. This, however, would have enabled the Spanish to dominate the Roussillon plain below, so much bickering ensued. Clause forty-two of the final Treaty ceded the Cerdagne to Spain *except* the valley of Latour de Carol, and *'thirty three villages'* on the Cerdagne plateau proper. This in effect handed half the plain to the French, and provided defensible ground, but as if often the way with legalitites, it left loopholes.

The treaty distinctly said *villages*, and the town of Llivia,

115

although surrounded by several of the thirty-three villages and their lands, was still a *town*. It had a charter and so, the Spanish successfully maintained, was excluded from the Treaty by the very provisions the French themselves had insisted upon. This caused such confusion that Cardinal Mazarin and the Spanish representative published *'An Explanation of the Forty Second Article of the Treaty of the Pyrénées'*, which granted Llivia to Spain. And so it remains, and Llivia is a Spanish enclave well within the frontiers of France. It says much for the good sense of both countries and the local people that this anomaly has endured for over three hundred years and caused no perceptible friction.

\*   \*   \*

Although Puigcerda is the historic capital of the Cerdagne, or, as the Catalans have it, the *Cerdenya,* this lies within Spain, so the true frontier town on our side of the border is Bourg Madame.

This little village has spent much of its history as a smuggling centre, and earned its living by hiring out mules to transport goods, duty paid or not, across the frontier. It was originally called La Guingetta and gained its present name in 1815 when, after the final defeat of Napoleon, Madame Royale, the titular head of the Bourbon family, returned to France from Spain through the Cerdagne.

There are only two main roads across the Cerdagne. Both begin or end at Bourg Madam in the west and Mont Louis, named incidentally, and I suppose inevitably after Louis XIV, in the east, spanning the plateau and providing the route for a circular tour.

From Bourg Madam it is easy to make a circle of the region, and since it is scant twenty kilometres from one side of the valley to the other you can accomplish this on foot or by car in a very short space of time. But take time if you can for this is a place worth exploring.

In summer the Cerdagne is delightful, but as it is high the air can be crisp and cold. In April or May, when the snow relents, the Cerdagne is a field of flowers, crocus lay in swathes across the meadows and arbutus, lupins, oleander and rhododendron flourish, while in autumn the forests by Carlit are a picture.

The northern route towards Font Romeu skirts Llivia and takes

*Solar oven, Font Romeu*

you to Angoustrine. The church here is well worth visiting, and
here you can turn off towards Dorres and walk over to the lakes
around the *massif* of Mont Carlit. Angoustrine has a fine little
church with carvings dedicated to the exploits of the Chevalier St.
Martin, while Dorres has one of those rare and much venerated
Black Virgins, but the Cerdagne has many fine churches, and the
Roussillon plain even more, so we must not glut ourselves too early
with ancient sculpture and exotic *romanesque.*

Past the jumbled rocks of Tergassonne, you will arrive at the
modern resort of Font-Romeu. This is very modern indeed, for
when Belloc passed this way in the 1900s, he makes no mention of

117

such a place but concentrated instead on Odeillo, which lies just below.'

Font Romeu is today a spa, a tourist resort, and a ski centre. It also contains the *Centre National de Recherche Solaire,* or C.N.R.S. in the shape of a vast solar oven, which dominates the much more ancient buildings of Odeillo.

The construction of modern Font-Romeu, a word which means the 'pilgrim spring' in Catalan, began about 1920, but the place became well known in the 1960s when, because of its height, the French chose to train their Olympic athletes there for the Mexico Games. Mexico City also lies at 2000 metres, and in such matters the supply of oxygen is critical. This largely fruitless effort left Font Romeu with a useful legacy in the shape of hotels, swimming pools, sports centres, ice rinks and all sorts of outdoor facilities, and to recoup the investment, the promotion of the town as a ski and walking centre soon followed.

The area has scope for both downhill and cross country skiing in winter, while in summer it swarms with walkers who swiftly disperse themselves into the surrounding mountains and across the Carlit massif. The mountains to the north are full of little lakes, some natural, some, like Bouillouses, dammed at one end to make a reservoir. The T.C.F. have a large summer hostel at Bouillouses, which serves walkers on the GR.10, and the circuit from Carlit to Bouillouses and so back to Font Romeu via the Col del Pam is a beautiful walk.

\*　　\*　　\*

Most of the villages between Font Romeu are ski centres, but Odeillo is different, and truly Catalan.

The Romansque church, protected by a cattle grill to keep animals out of church, shelters the Virgin of Font Romeu, the *Vierge de l'Invention.*

The Roussillon of which the Cerdagne forms a part, is a shrine to the Romanesque, a word which has nothing to do with the Romans but refers to the *romantic* or imaginative carvings with which otherwise simple churches are embellished. The style is roughly contemporary with the Norman architecture of England, and died

118

out when the development of the pointed arch enabled architects to design walls higher and thinner and develop the 'Gothic' style.

This particular Virgin, at Odeillo, was supposedly discovered by a bull, and is the centre for much local veneration, spending its time between the church at Odeillo and the chapel at l'Hermitage, above Font Romeu.

The bull, when unearthing the Virgin, also discovered a spring, the water of which was said to cause miraculous cures, and this, too, brought pilgrims to the church which, like so many Romanesque buildings, is small, dark and solidly built. After the modern lights of Font Romeu and the futuristic solar oven nearby, this is a place to see, just for the contrast.

Mount Louis at the head of the valley, is a bastion, fortified by Vauban in case the Treaty of the Pyrénées ever wavered. When describing the site to Louis XIV he listed the hard climate found there as a defensive feature. Certainly Mont Louis is a chilly spot, a garnerer of storms. It commands all the routes out of the valley to the north and east. Vauban, who left his mark on all the frontiers of France as military architect to Louis XIV, built Mont Louis about 1679, and it proved its worth during the early Revolutionary wars of the following century. General Dagobert held it against the Spanish and used it to launch the counter attack which drove the Bourbon forces from the Cerdagne. Mont Louis is still a considerable fortress with very few inhabitants apart from the garrison, usually comprised of reluctant conscripts.

\*     \*     \*

The road back to the west towards Bourg Madam has some interesting villages along the way and, apart from the skiing on the slopes of Puigmal and the Cambras d'Aze, is much less developed and therefore (to my mind anyway) much more attractive.

Eyne, or Planes, on the GR.10, are good centres for walking to the *cirque* at Cambras, and from here you can see south to the Sierra del Cadi, and on a clear day towards Canigou. There is a good trek of three or four days from Eyne to Canigou, crossing the frontier to Nuria, and after Urr passing through Mantet, without losing much height, and so up the steep side of Canigou and over to Prades.

119

The church at Planes is triangular, an apparently Romanesque building with bell-tower and barrel-vault. Some claim that it dates from the Arab Conquest and was once a mosque, but most probably it gained its present shape simply by occasional enlargement.

The Cerdagne, as we noticed when we arrived at Porté, is as much a basin as a plateau, and this rim around Puigmal is threaded by several valleys coming down from the south, each with a village at its foot.

The Segre, which runs into Llo, is a tributary of the Ebro, and runs through a narrow gorge above the village on the slopes of Puigmal. This village contains another *Atalaye* or watch tower, and a Romanesque church where the door is quite unique, decorated with symbols picked out in nail heads.

Saillagouse is just a little place, with one excellent little hotel, the *Auberge Atalaya*, in a farmhouse just above the village. If you prefer something a little more chic, the *Auberge d'Eyne* is one of the Relais et Chateaux hotels, and offers a large *Gastronomique* menu and a very warm welcome. These hotels, and the *Hôtel Planes,* which is another excellent auberge in Saillagouse, serve the skiers of Puigmal and a considerable number of lucky summer visitors.

If you turn south before Hix you can make a little tour towards Osseje, and on foot in summer or on skis in winter, get up to the crête, overlooking the frontier. The views can be spectacular although this is a terrible place in winter when the wind cuts across the lip of the hills and rushes down the valley, forcing you back, plastered with snow, into the shelter of the trees.

Hix is the former capital of the Counts of the Cerdagne in the decades before they came into money and took themselves off to Puigcerda. It is a quaint little village with a fine Romanesque church, and inside you will find several treasures, a retable of St. Martin with the Virgin, dating from about 1400, and a series of saintly images including one of St. Helen, mother of Constantine, whom we shall meet again at Elne.

\*    \*    \*

There are four exits from the Cerdagne. Two we have already

120

seen, one to the west through Puymorens, another south to Spain through Puigcerda. At the eastern end of the valley are two more, one to the north towards Quillan down the valley of the Capcir, and the other down the sweeping road, beside the railway line which carries *le petit train jaune* to the Conflent. One leads to the Valley of the Aude, the other to the Roussillon plain, and both are places we will visit later since they can be linked up, but let us explore both exits as we return to the valley floor.

The Capcir is a narrow valley carved out by the River Aude which rises in the Cerdagne and runs through woods and rocks down to the main valley at Quillan. Just after leaving Mont Louis, a forest track on the right leads up to Bouillouses and you can walk up here past the lakes and on to Carlit. All this is green forest, excellent walking and skiing country and full of wildlife, notably the izard, the chamois of the Pyrénées which like to browse on the young saplings.

Formiguères, which lies below the vast reservoir at Matemale was once the hunting lodge for the Kings of Aragon and is the true capital of the Capcir, in spite of its size. King Sancho of Majorca died here in 1324. The houses are tiny with thick walls, and sheltering among the trees, for the winter snows lie long and heavy here for much of the year. The river is dammed again at Puyvalador, another small village, which officially marks the end of the true Capcir, and the start of the Aude gorges. These were sealed by the château of Usson, now in ruins, and you can turn off here to the Donezan and Ax past the Cathar fortress of Quérigut, but the gorges on the main road are narrow and spectacular, with heavy rocks overhanging the road until you come to the straggling village of Axat and, back on the main road, through the even more imposing Defile de Pierre Lys, until you arrive at Quillan.

\*     \*     \*

The eastern exit from Mont Louis is equally spectacular. The Haut Conflent is one of those places which, for good or ill, are places of passage. You rush through them from one place to another and never think to stop, particularly when the road is steep and narrow. The Conflent is like this, and being divided into two parts, *Haut et Basse,* it sees many travellers but few visitors.

The high valley runs from Mont Louis down to the Vauban fortress of Villefranche-de-Conflent. There you are in the lower valley and may then proceed on side trips to such places as Vernet les Bains, or the Romanesque abbeys of St. Martin du Canigou or at St. Michel de Cuxa, above Prades.

The road down from the Cerdagne is notable for severe curves, and the sight of two fine bridges, the Pont Guiscard, named after the man who built it and died in the process, and the Pont Séjourne, again named after its builder, the chief engineer of the *département.*

These bridges are crossed by the *petit train jaune,* which will whisk you from the Cerdagne, and the section from Mont Louis down to little Olette is the most spectacular of the whole journey.

Villefranche de Conflent should be a *bastide* and in a sense it is, built primarily to seal the lower exit from the Cerdagne. It is completely enclosed by the walls built by Vauban, and stands at the junction of the Têt, one of the three great rivers of Roussillon, and its tributary, the Cady.

Villefranche was built by the Kings of Aragon after the Treaty of Corbeil in 1258 drew up the boundary between the French and Spanish Kingdoms, and fixed the frontier of Aragon on the Corbières.

The Porte d'Espagne still carries the machinery of the drawbridge, and even to modern eyes, this is a formidable town and as such not particularly attractive. You feel that this looks like St. Jean Pied de Port ought to look. The old château, reached — so they say — by nine hundred and ninety nine steps, towers above the town, and served Louis XIV as a prison, although it is now a private house and cannot be visited.

A wander around Villefranche can be a chilling experience in more ways than one, for this is a true Vauban fortress and has few opportunities to charm the visitor, and the wind from the mountains whips about the streets. The church of St. Jacques is late Romanesque with some Gothic, and contains some interesting medieval carvings, but this town is a citadel and little else, imposing and even a little menacing. There are, however, some pleasing sites in the other valley to the south, along the Cady. The Counts of the Cerdagne built a castle at Corneilla, which has virtually disappeared, but their church is magnificent.

*Pont Séjourne*

Vernet, although now a spa, is a fine little town with views over Canigou, and from here we can descend past St. Michael du Cuxa to the plains of Roussillon, saying goodbye for a while anyway, to the grey-green mountains, and passing through the doorway on to the plains of Roussillon.

# 8 · Roussillon

Roussillon, the red land, is the home of the French Catalans. The heart of their homeland is the vast flat wine-drenched coastal plain which sprawls out below Canigou, and is centred on the capital of the province, Perpignan, a fine, historic and attractive city not far from the coast.

However we descend from the Cerdagne, we will eventually arrive in the Conflent, and the valley of the Têt, one of the three great rivers of Roussillon, the others being the Agly to the north, and the Tech, which circles from behind Canigou to the south. All flow out into the Mediterranean and water the coastal plain.

The valley of the Têt is a paradise in the early summer, for this is fruit country, a shock of blossom from peach and apricot. They call this land of Roussillon the *pays de quatre saisons*, and you can find all climates here in the space of a day, winter on the heights, autumn on the slopes, spring in the valleys, and summer by the sea.

Prades, capital of the area, has a *sous-prefecture,* and is quite a busy little town with several fine restaurants, notably the *Hostalrich,* or the smaller *Hôtel de La Poste* in the Rue Château dun.

The church of St. Pierre dominates the central square, and the inside of the church is mastered in turn by a vast retable behind the altar, the work of Sunyer in the mid-17th century. Personally, I was more intrigued by the street called *Impasse des Neuf Fiances,* just off the main road. Here, some time in the reign of Charles V, all the local lads were engaged at the same time. It can't happen very often and the name lives on.

Prades is surrounded by mountains and overlooked by the Canigou massif, which is frequently veiled in clouds. Only in winter, when the air is crisp, can you be sure of seeing Canigou, the mystery mountain of the Catalans, rearing up from the surrounding plain.

Until he died, in 1973, Prades was the home of the great 'cellist, Pablo Casals. He organised music festivals in his adopted home town and the little place became quite famous, although the concerts once held here have since been translated to the monastery of St. Michel de Cuxa on the slopes of Canigou, which can be easily visited from Prades.

Roussillon, thanks to the fact that it was a mainly Spanish or rather an Aragonese possession, with interruptions, until as late as 1659, resisted the Gothic influence of the Ile de France and so retains all that is best of the Romanesque. The earliest Romanesque art in France is the lintel over the door at St. Génis des Fontaines, south of Elne, and that is just a *soupçon* of all the Romanesque architecture for which Roussillon is famous.

In period, and in certain styles, Romanesque is similar to Norman architecture in England, but although the name comes from the 'Romantic' nature of the carvings with which the best of these strong sturdy buildings are usually embellished, these carvings were offered by way of compensation. Early builders could not fathom out how to bridge the vault. To support the roof they used rounded arches and thick walls, which would be weakened by windows. The windows were therefore small and the glory of such buildings rested with the masons who made up for architectural limitations by embellishing the cloisters. With the discovery that a well-pitched roof and a pointed arch could rest on thinner walls, the Romanesque gave way, at least in the Ile de France, to the grey glory of Gothic, but you may enjoy hereabouts the more solid Romanesque style. The monastery at St. Michel de Cuxa is therefore a necessary stop, as is its neighbour, St. Martin's

126

*St Michel de Cuxa*

monastery high on nearby Canigou, which can be reached, with some effort, from Vernet.

St. Michel was built by the Benedictines in about 878, and grew in fame until the Wars of Religion, when it was wrecked. It once sheltered as a simple monk, Pietro Orseolo, a noted Doge of Venice. The cloister has been much despoiled, and some of the pillars have gone away as far as America. You will see many of the others on the west front of the church at Prades. The abbey fell into ruin after the Revolution, but has now returned to the Benedictines and serves again as church and cultural centre.

The road from St. Michel leads up to Taurinya and another magnificent Romanesque abbey, St. Martin du Canigou, which has to be reached on foot. This dates from about 1000 AD and the beauty of the architecture is enhanced by the position. The cloister has again been despoiled, but the crypt and chapel of 'Our Lady Under Ground' is still intact. It was built by Guifred, the tenth Count of the Cerdagne, and his tomb, which he built himself, is in the gardens.

From St. Martin's you can climb on up to the Canigou peak at 2784m., with magnificent views back over the abbey, but the best route up is from Vernet, up the little road to the *Chalet-Hôtel* at Cortalet. People stay there overnight, and rise while it is still dark to see the dawn from the top, rising to the east, across the sea. If the clouds are scanty, and they often are in the early morning, the views are superb, and I have seen sunset over Canigou where the colours begger description.

Canigou is a popular route today, but it was not in fact climbed regularly until the last century, although Peter III of Aragon attempted it in 1285. The summit is supposed to be the haunt of witches, and it is bleak enough when the clouds gather to welcome a host of covens. Canigou is the pride of the Catalans, and they glorify their mountain in song and story, so that the mountain often hides its blushes in cloud. Whatever the witches have to do with it, seen from the plain on a clear blue day, snow-topped Canigou is a magnificent mountain.

\*     \*     \*

West of Mount Canigou lie the foothills of the Aspres, an

*Hermitage, Notre Dame del Coll*

outcrop of the Pyrénées. Overshadowed by the mountain they may be, but let them not be overlooked. On the way there from the Conflent you will see, away on your left, the hill-town of Eus, across the Têt, and a little way past you turn off right, across the Aspres hills, towards Amelie-les-Bain. Eus looks ancient but dates largely from the last 200 years, creeping up the hill as the population grew.

These empty hills, indeed all the lonely parts of Roussillon are dotted with small chapels, or hemitages, many dating from 1000 AD or thereabouts, and all fascinating. Most are dedicated to Our Lady, *Notre Dame,* and you will find them everywhere. I try to be selective in my choice of churches, but this route across the Aspres includes three you must not miss.

The priory at Serrabonne, really a small monastery, is another place to arrive at on foot up a winding track. It is a lonely place, silent in the green hills, but the carving on the arches of the nave is

129

quite remarkable, a blaze of pink and gold, and the purest Romanesque. You must time your visit with care, for the church is only open between 10 am. and 12 noon, and from 2 pm. to 5 pm., but you must go there.

Further along the road to Amelie is yet another little church, the Chapel of La Trinite, consecrated in 953 by the Bishop of Elne. This has a remarkable 12th-century iron-studded door, filched from the ruined castle of Belpuig on the hill above, while in the church itself, reeking of wax from a score of candles, you will discover a 12th century retable of the Trinity, and a Byzantine crucifix.

Turning here west, across and over the hills, a rough road will take you to another pilgrim hermitage, remote Notre Dame del Coll, now deserted and desecrated, with sweeping views over the valley to the Roussillon plain, and so, via Thuir, where they manufacture *Byrrh,* my least favourite *aperitif,* to Castelnou, a veritable gem.

\*     \*     \*

Castelnou is a walled town. The 11th century castle dominates the town, and the houses hug its walls, a network of steep cobbled alleys giving you access to the interior. At the top of the town you will discover little shops and at least one excellent restaurant, *L'Oustal*, where you can enjoy a true Catalan *cargolade*, a spicey dish of grilled snails.

The little town dates from about 1000 AD, when the castle was constructed, and has to join that list of places which everyone should visit in Roussillon.

Thuir was once prettier than it is today, but there are interesting places in the countryside round about. South of Thuir, you arrive at the lovely Monastir del Camp, a priory marking the spot where a Christian army of Charlemagne, battling with thirst as well as the Saracens, were saved from defeat by the sudden, miraculous appearance of spring.

St. Génis des Fontaines has one great claim to our attention. The church is, as usual, Romanesque, but the tympanum over the door is a remarkable example of Romanesque art in its own right and is said to be the earliest example of the Romanesque in France. This,

130

*Lintel, St Genis des Fontaines*

as far as we know, is where it all began. The church dates from 819 and the lintel, which shows Christ in Majesty, is dedicated to Robert the Pious, King of France — or more exactly, the Ile de France, who ruled in about the year 1000. The carving was ordered by the Abbot of the monastery which once stood there.

The undiscovered Aspres are full of such little gems and you must tour about and find them along the minor roads below the Canigou, before moving into Amélie on the Tech, and heading for the Vallespir. The Romans came to the springs here and called it *Aquae Calidae*. The present town is named from the Queen of that unlucky monarch, Louis-Philippe, and is the perfect example of a Pyrénean spa.

*    *    *

Céret in the Vallespir is famous for its bridge across the Tech, built by the Devil (or so they say) and restored in the 14th century.

131

Céret is a centre for fruit growing, so go there in March to see the trees laden with blossom, or a little later to enjoy the fruit; cherries, peaches, apricots, every tree bowed under with the weight of the crop.

Céret is also a centre for the arts and was the home in their day of such painters as Braque, Picasso, and Juan Gris, who all lived here at the turn of the century. There is also a fine war memorial by the Catalan sculptor, Maillot, and you will see his work all over Roussillon.

West again, up the Vallespir, beyond Amélie the road takes you to Arles. This has, just for a change, a Gothic cloister in St. Sauveur's, and is the place to turn south for St. Laurent de Cerdens, and Coustouges. This little road peters out below the frontier. At St. Laurent they make *espadrilles*, (which always give me blisters) while Coustouges is a real frontier town, and overlooks the valleys of Spain. It has a vast church and miniscule congregation, but the real reason for going there is to explore the other foothills of the Roussillon, the Albères which complete the Pyrénées journey to the sea at Port-Vendres.

Down the main road lies Prats-de-Mollo, another frontier town, and inevitably one structured by Vauban. The walled upper town once held a hunting lodge for the Kings of Aragon, and the Spanish frontier is a mere nine miles away. The valley is wider here, and the word *'prat'* is Catalan, of course, and means a 'meadow'. Prats has a huge church dating from 482 AD and is a great centre for walking, as is the entire Vallespir. If you head south towards Spain you can come to yet another hermitage, Notre Dame du Coral, once the centre for a local pilgrimage. If this is too far, try another walk to nearby St. Pierre de Reuferrier, a Romanesque chapel with a high beil tower.

Back down the valley a side road runs to Montferrier, and the Gorges of La Fou, while another runs up to Corsavy, well up on Canigou. Both places are hill towns, bleak in winter, barely below the snowline, but beautiful at any time.

\* \* \*

The Albères hills are the last gasp of the Pyrénées, and they run into the sea at last near Banyuls. Many minor roads run into them, but there is poor lateral communication here except on foot. The Atlantic-Mediterranean footpath, the GR.10, runs across the Albères and can be followed down to the coast from Prats, a distance of some forty miles.

Above Céret you will find, on a windy hill, a memorial to the *Evades,* commemorating those soldiers, airmen, escaped prisoners of war, and Resistance fighters who made thier painful way across these hills into Spain during the Second World War, while beyond Boulou, lies Sorede, a place to chart the course of the Romanesque. The church has another Romanesque lintel, like the one at St. Génis, but this dates from about 100 years later, and the decoration inside the church is already considerably more refined. The whole Albères range is worth exploring, and these little villages, while worth a visit, are also pegs to hang your travels on as we run out to the East.

Beyond Sorède lies the sea, which we reach at Argelès, the northern town of the Côte Vermeille, some two hundred and fifty miles from the Côte Basque.

*　　*　　*

Roussillon lies on the Gulf of Lions, and the coast can be conveniently divided into two arcas, which run north and south of Argelès. North of Argelès the coast is flat and sandy all the way to Barcarès on the Languedoc frontier, a distance of about twenty miles. To the south, as far as the frontier with Spain, the coast is rocky, though with sandy bays, and the south is, to my mind, much more interesting.

The pearl of the Côte Rochèuse is Collioure, a fortified fishing village with a mighty castle built by the Knights Templar, walls by Vauban, and a beautiful church with a roof plated with pink tiles attributed to the Romans. The harbour has two good beaches, and the *quais* are backed by many restaurants, while within the walls the dining room of the *Hôtel des Templiers* is hung with the works of Matisse, Derain and Picasso, who stayed there and paid for their food with their work. In summer Collioure is very, very crowded, but you will have to go there for the real flavour of the Catalan coast, and, if you are wise, to eat lunch at *La Bodega*.

The hills behind Collioure grow grapes for the red wine and

aperitif of Banyuls, and as a choice for your excursions you have either the hermitage of Notre Dame de Consolation, or the brooding bulk of the Tour Madeloc. These Albères hills, close to the frontier which, you will recall, lay to the north, are dotted with watchtowers and fortresses, erected against the French and the ever-hovering Corsairs from the Barbary coast.

Below Collioure, a real seaman's haunt, lies Port Vendres. This appears modern and decidedly under-employed, but the Romans used it, and called it *Portus Veneris*, the Port of Venus. The restaurants behind the port serve excellent fish soups and *bouillabaisse,* at prices considerably lower than those demanded in popular Collioure.

*Church and tower, Collioure*

From Port Vendres it is a short dash to the frontier at Port Bou, past Banyuls, heavy with wine, and home of the Arago Aquarium, so let us turn north again, first to Elne, and so up to the capital of Roussillon, the great town of Perpignan.

\*　　\*　　\*

Elne is old, curious, overlooked. Before the sea retreated, Elne was a port, the harbour of Pyrene for the Ligurian tribes, six hundred years before the birth of Christ. Pliny wrote about it as a safe haven for seamen. This town stood on the road Hercules followed, seeking the apples of Hesperides, which if they ever existed were simply oranges.

Hannibal drove his elephants through here, marching to the Second Punic War, and later on the first Christian Emperor of Rome, Constantine, began the Church here and named the town *Castrum Helenae,* after his mother Helen. You will find Constantine's symbol, the *Labarum*, carved on a wall in the cloister.

The church at Elne is magnificent, by far the largest and finest in Roussillon, with finely carved pillars in the cloister and a number of tombs. The building dates from the 11th century, and though ravaged by time and the wars, especially by Phillip the Bold in 1285, the structure has been well preserved.

\*　　\*　　\*

Perpignan lies on the Roussillon plain, encircled by eternal vineyards and dominated by the red brick castle and palace of the Kings of Majorca. Perpignan is quite large, with over a hundred thousand inhabitants, and ranks as the second city after Barcelona in this heartland of the Catalans.

The present centre of Perpignan lies at the Castillet, a red brick fortress begun in 1368, which was once a bastion on the ramparts, later a prison, and is now a museum. From here you can wander into the back streets and up just a little way to the cafes by the Place de la Loge. Here, in the evenings from June to September they dance the *Sardane,* the sprightly unforgettable folk dance of Catalonia. Folk groups start the dance, and the customers rise from

*The Castillet, Perpignan*

their tables outside the cafes and join in, circling and swaying to that wonderful, lilting music. The nicest thing about the *Sardane* is that it is truly a people's dance and everyone joins in. I have since discovered that this facility is due to the fact that they teach it in school. Also, to my considerable chagrin, I have since learned that the *Sardane* is not an old dance and seems to have originated in Barcelona in about 1860.

The *Loge de Mer,* just off the *Place*, is a very fine medieval building which was once the seat of a tribunal governing the maritime interests of Catalonia, fixing rates, making treaties, and chastising pirates. The courtyard of the Loge contains a very fine statue by Aristide Maillol, the noted Catalan sculptor. Maillol's wife served as a model for many of his nudes and, as you will clearly see, she was a fine figure of a woman.

The church of St. Jean is a huge building begun in 1325 by Sancho, the second King of Majorca. This is a Gothic structure with some Romansque chapels and is not dissimilar to the great cathedral of Palma de Mallorca. The church contains several interesting sights including effiges of Sancho, and the tomb of Bishop Louis de Montmort. To the side of the church stands another little chapel dating from 1025, containing a remarkable carving of the crucifixion, the emaciated *'devot'* Christ. This shows the Passion in all its agony, and is a startling work of art. It dates from 1529, is probably Spanish, and the feet are washed with wine every Ash Wednesday.

If you carry on wandering through the streets you will come to the Musée Rigaud, which among other treasures, contains works by the painter Hycinthe Rigaud, court painter to Louis XIV, and a native of Perpignan. Nearby is the church of St. Jacques, dedicated to the saint of Compostella. This is a base for the sect of the *Confrerie de la Sanch,* a religious group which, cloaked and hooded in red, like apprentices of the dreaded Inquisition, parade the town in Holy Week. Their processional cross, hung with the symbols of the Passion is suspended in the porch.

The great Castle and Palace of the Kings of Majorca dominates the town. The palace, which lies in the centre of the fortress, is itself quite small, and the ancient rooms, the *Sala de Mallorca*, or the *Sala de Timbres*, the Hall of Seals, now houses a Catalan museum. I have attended concerts in the courtyard here, when the

*Maillol Statue, Loge, Perpignan*

Orchestra de Barcelona came up to play in the second city, hoping in vain that the performance would not be scoured by the ever watchful *tramontane*. The *tramontane* is the great wind which flays this coast, and is, indeed the one snag. They say that if it blows for three days it will blow for six, and if for six, then nine . . . Even one day is wearing.

Perpignan has all the attributes of a capital city, a Palais de Congress, many hotels, magnificent public buildings, and fine restaurants. I recommend the *'Francois Villon'* near the cathedral of St. Jean, *Le Lyonnaise* on the boulevard, the *Relais de Clairfont* on the road towards Thuir, or *La Racasse* at nearby Canet-Plage. Roussillon food and wine is always good, and the seafood is superb.

\* \* \*

By now we have come a long way. The green Atlantic surely still beats on the Basque coast, even while the beaches here are washed by a blue sea but is seems hard to believe it. The green Basque country is so very different from the red and gold of Roussillon.

This is a good moment to look back across the spine of the Pyrénées, that great dramatic and historic range of hills. Mountains are so often a barrier, but the Pyrénées are a link, joining France and Spain, the Catalans and the Basques, while sheltering within those many valleys we have visited, and the many more we have missed, many fine people and some unique history.

We must turn away from them now, into yet another range of hills, to Salses on the frontiers of Roussillon, and into the Corbiérés. There are the little hills of the Pyrénées but they repay inspection.

# 9 · The Corbières

The Corbières are the foothills of the Eastern Pyrénées, circling the Roussillon plain to the north. Like most foothills they are overshadowed by the mountain range beyond, but the Corbières are worth exploring, and contain within their tucks and folds a host of fascinating places.

The Corbières is first and foremost wine country. Every valley, every flat stone-fringed terrace is thickly green with vines. Until quite recently the wines of the Corbières were more noted for their quantity than their quality, and awarded a charitable VDQS. Then, after the French withdrew from Algeria, many settlers, the so-called *Pieds-noirs,* settled in the south and applied their skills to improving the local wine. Intensive cultivation, a policy of improving the vines and introducing fresh strains is starting to show results, and the VDQS is now well earned. Certain growths are even being elevated to the more prestigious *appelation contrôlée,* so you may rest assured that in the Corbières at least you won't go thirsty.

This chapter then is something of a wine tour, and why not? I enjoy wine but like many people, cannot afford the great vintages. Besides, they are now considerably overpriced and in a country which produces so much wine it is not difficult to find wines which are very palatable and none the worse for being unknown to fame, and less than wildly expensive.

*     *     *

The Corbières occupy a wide region west of the coastal road which runs north from Perpignan to Narbonne. The country, a rolling network of hills, runs west as far as the Valley of the Aude, a river which swings east at Carcassonne and provides the northern boundary for these hills separating the Corbières from the Minervois.

If we begin just north of Perpignan, we can start at Riversaltes, a little town famous for its *aperitif* and for Marshal Joffre, a stolid soldier of the Great War, and the victor of Marne. Joffre remained as Commander in Chief of the French Armies for two years, impervious to the assaults of the Germans, the pleas of his Allies and the losses among his own men, until Verdun overwhelmed him. He sank into national obscurity to make way for Petain, the victor of Verdun, and, in the next war, the unfortunate leader of Vichy.

The flatlands between Rivesaltes and the sea, the *Salanque,* is interesting, a paradise for birds and seamed with streams, tributaries of the river Agly. On the ponds, pink flamingoes wade, and egrets peck away among the reed beds.

In the spring, after the rain, the rivers are high and the mosquitoes are plentiful, but in summer the land throbs under the sun, and the air shimmers with heat. The *Hôtel Les Pin* at St. Laurent de La Salanque is an excellent place to stay in when visiting this region, and serves local food and nearby lies the great fortress of Salses.

By now my liking for castles must be well established and it might be advisable for me to select my castles as carefully as I choose my churches. A surfeit of either could be boring. Salses though is different, and as there are few castles like it anywhere in Europe, this one should be visited.

The most striking thing about the château-fort of Salses is its colour. It is a warm red, tinted with green and yellow, a solid hunk of brick, massive in construction, half concealed behind its deep *fosse.*

*Castle of Salses*

What you see here is the finest example of the *transitional* castle in all Europe. It was built for the Catholic sovereigns of Spain, in about 1497, by a Catalan architect, Ramirez. He built his castle to match the age of cannon, and when the great Vauban came to inspect Salses nearly two hundred years later, he found nothing worth changing, although, having thought it over he changed the castle considerably.

Salses has sloping walls and *glacis* to deflect cannon balls, and flat gun platforms to permit the defenders' cannon a full arc of fire. Every defensible point is linked with its neighbours so that the deep ditch was covered with a crossfire, and deep arrow or musket slits command the closer approaches.

Once you cross the drawbridge and enter the courtyard and intact buildings, you will find at Salses a complete frontier fortress, with garrison quarters, dungeons and *oubliettes*.

143

And, in the end, it was all for nothing. Salses never saw action. It served as a prison and has been almost demolished several times. Now it sits there, a reminder of warlike days, the last, and first castle of Roussillon.

*    *    *

Estagel is a wine town, a centre for the *Côtes de Roussillon,* but is chiefly famous as the birthplace of the Roussillon's most famous son, Dominuque-François Arago, who was born here in 1786. He was a scientist and a politician, and you will find statues and buildings named in his honour all over the Roussillon. Today, Estagel is undistinguished, but the local wines of the *Côtes du Roussillon* are coming on nicely. They are *appelation contrôlée,* and those of the Château de Jau, of Rasiguères and, my particular favourite, from the little walled village of Latour-de-France, are excellent and very reasonably priced.

There is a network of minor roads threading this area, where every village has a *cave,* a region overlooked to the south by the bulk of Canigou and to the north by the line of the Fénouilledes. This is a tall escarpment just under 1000 metres high and once marked the boundary of Aragon and the *comté* of Tolouse. When the French kings took over this frontier they decided to reinforce this natural barrier with a string of fortresses, garrisoned from the Cité of Carcassonne, and in the 12th and 13th centuries, the 'sons of Carcassone' rose to mark and guard the demesne of the French, and keep out the Spanish.

There are seven of them. Aguilar, the castle of the eagle, near Tuchan, Quéribus near Maury, once a Cathar fortress which is now being restored, as is nearby Peyrepertuse. Mighty Puilaurens looms up near Axat, while Quérigut, as we have seen, plugs the road from the Cerdagne, and the western roads from Ariège.

The last two, Puivert and Termes, are off this natural defensive line. Puivert lies in the Ariège, while Termes lies in the centre of the Corbières and was undoubtedly designed as a supporting line and an outpost of Carcassonne, the great fortress *cité* of the region.

*    *    *

*The Fenouillèdes*

It is important to remember that throughout the Medieval period, the Franco-Spanish frontier lay *north* of the Pyrénées. Their châteaux forts were made obsolete, not just by gunpowder, but by the southward march of the frontier, and the present decay of the castles is due more to local people borrowing their dressed stone to build houses than to enemy action. They are spectacular and Aguilar, Quéribus and Puilaurens in particular are magnificent castles, crowning their respective heights and giving those visitors who pant and scramble on to their warlike ramparts, a breathtaking view over the surrounding countryside. I confess that I like castles, and no fosse, wall or tower will go uninspected if time permits.

145

Reason tells me that they were places of fearful conflict and repression, but romance reminds me of the days of chivalry . . .

*When every morning brought a noble chance,*
*And every chance brought out a noble Knight*

\* \* \*

There are two ways in to the Corbières through the Fenouilledes. You can climb over the Col St. Louis and then turn east for Bugarach, or pass through St. Paul and up the gorges of Galamus.

St. Paul was once a centre for the manufacture of pipes and it is said that briar pipes were invented here — the name coming from the local name for the scrub, *bruyère*, from the roots of which the pipe bowls were made.

This scrub, or *garrigue,* as they call it in the Languedoc, is fearsome stuff. In the summer it becomes tinder dry and virtually explodes at the touch of a careless match. Huge fires sweep these hills every summer and the damage they do takes years to repair. On my last trip the hills north of Galamus were quite barren, with weary road gangs replacing yet again the telephone cables, drawing out the burnt poles like blackened teeth from the charred ground. This land needs and cannot get an adequate rainfall. When it does rain the scents are marvellous, but more often the hills shimmer dustily in the heat, ready to rise up roaring and punish the land, at the first touch of flame.

The gorges of Galamus are famous and that is a snag. The road which edges its way through, circling the sheer side of the ravine, is wide enough for only one car at a time, and the passing places are inadequate. Creeping from one to the other takes quite a while, but it does give the visitor time to get out and peer into the depths. The Agly foams a thousand feet below, and proves that when it comes to making its mark on the land it can show the Aude and even the mighty Tarn a thing or two.

\* \* \*

Michelin describes the Corbières as the *rampart of Languedoc,* and indeed once you have passed through the gorges of Galamus you are out of Roussillon. The red and gold stripes of the Catalans

146

are replaced by the gold cross on a red field of Languedoc, ancient banner of the Counts of Toulouse.

At Cubières, north of the gorge, you can turn either way, skirting the "Sons of Carcassonne," and head for Durban and the wine country of Fitou. Languedoc wines exceed those of Roussillon in quantity but not quality, but the wines of Fitou are A.C., *appellation contrôlée,* and very drinkable. Most of the Corbières wines are red, and are frequently sold as a wine to blend with other wines, into drinkable house 'plonk'. The local people consume it in large amounts, and a consumption of several litres per day by a working man is by no means uncommon. How they manage it I cannot imagine.

Travelling north-east across the Corbières, past Durban, you will eventually come to one of the great attractions of the region, the abbey of Fontfroide. This was built by the Cistercians in about the year 1050, and is tucked away in the Valley of the Gue, not far from Narbonne. It has for many years been in private hands, but it is open to visitors and the cloister, which has been lovingly restored, is said to be the most beautiful in Southern France.

The Corbières is not a populated region, and has no great restaurants, but the *Broche au Bois* at Roquefort, south of Fontfroide is a worthy stop and serves local dishes.

Lagrasse, west of Frontfroide, is a small *bastide.* I like little out-of-the-way places and for this purpose Lagrasse is ideal. The abbey was founded by Charlemagne, and fortified during the wars of the Albigensians and then continually rebuilt until the 18th century. The village has much of the former fortifications, and is built on the *bastide* plan, a delightful spot to pause in on a hot summer day.

\*     \*     \*

Finally, our route to the north lies down again to Quillan and the Valley of the Aude. We left the Aude at Axat, at the foot of the Capcir. From there it rushes north towards Carcassone and through glorious country, but let us stop at Couiza, and hear a strange tale. Above Couiza, high on a hill, lies the little village of Rennes-le-Château, and here lies a great mystery.

At the end of the last century the little village of Rennes-le-Chateau obtained a new cure for its little Romanesque church, one Bérengar Saunière. Saunière was a local man, born near Couiza.

He took up his living in 1885, and served in this lonely spot, as poor as his own church mice, until, sometime in 1893 Saunière found something. What is was, and how he did it is still a subject of much heated debate, but almost overnight Saunière became fantasically rich. Money oozed from his hilltop village, building houses, paving the road up from Couiza — a road soon travelled by a host of people far removed from the present and *petit bourgoise* of the Aude valley.

Actresses, philosophers, people of less than savoury reputation flocked to Rennes and were royally entertained.

As to where the money for all this came from, Saunière flatly refused to say, even when fetched before the Bishop's Court in Carcassonne. So, in the absence of explanation, strange tales arose. Some say that he chanced on the treasure of the Jews, which the Romans failed to find when Jerusalem fell in 70AD. Others say that he chanced on the lost treasure of the Cathars, that *"gold, silver and a great quantity of money"* which went over the wall of Montségur one wild hopeless night in 1244 and was never seen again. Yet another tale says that when Jacques de Molay, doomed Master of the Knights Templar arrived in France in 1308 he brought with him the moveable treasure of the Order, fifty mule-loads of gold. After trial and torture Molay went to the stake in Paris, but no one has ever found the fabulous treasure of the Templars. Or did Saunière?

However, if the source is hearsay, Saunière's wealth is undisputed and so is the mystery which surrounds him. He spent lavishly until his death in 1917, refusing to leave his little village even after the Council of Bishops at Carcassonne had him unfrocked. When Saunière died his secret and his wealth died with him. His housekeeper kept her silence too, dying in poverty, and both are buried in the stoney little graveyard behind the church . . . Ah yes, the church!

The church at Rennes is very old, Romanesque, and in some disrepair. Saunière carried out a great deal of rebuilding and had the church redecorated in the strangest fashion, and the whole place gives even the most stolid visitor shudders of dismay.

You will need a key to get in, but even before you enter, the lintel above the door will strike you as unusual, carved with the legend *"Terriblis est locus ste"* — which means "This place is terrible"!

Once inside you see why. The Devil crouches under the holy water stoup, holding it up with long clawlike nails. Above, in a mural, Christ preaches to a small crowd, while, disregarded on the ground, behind them lies a bag of money. People say that the church at Rennes is full of clues to the source of Saunière's wealth, but whether that is so or not, the building is a depressing and evil place, and one you will be glad to leave.

The mystery of Rennes-le-Château goes beyond Saunière's wealth, however he came by it. It centres on the little church and on a history of rumours, of sorcery, black magic and violence. Those who search for Saunière's treasure are said to come to a violent end, and if this has never disuaded the searchers, the risk, vague as it is, still hangs in the air.

Down below, at Couiza, the sun is out and the Aude rushes over the rocks. Couiza has a delightful little fortress, and is the place to sample that sparkling wine of Languedoc, the *Blanquette de Limoux*. This is the party wine of the region, just the thing to dash away the vapours of Rennes-le-Château, before we press on to Carcassonne.

\*　　\*　　\*

From the ramparts of Carcassonne, you can look back to the Pyrénées, a small dark cloud floating on the southern horizon. All roads from the Eastern Pyrénées lead to Carcassonne, the great fortress town of the Counts of Toulouse, built to command the southern entrance to the great valley which runs up to Toulouse itself.

Carcassonne was the seat of the Trencavel family, vicounts who held their city from the St. Gilles family until the Albigensian Crusaders took the city in 1209.

Carcassonne was always a great fortress, which resisted the Black Prince and was modified and enlarged until the Treaty of the Pyrénées and cannon made it obsolete. By the early 19th century Carcassonne was a rat-infested ruin, but in 1835 Prosper Merimée, inspector of the Beaux-Arts who was charged with preserving the former glories of France, saw it. Would it not be a fine thing, he thought, to restore this place to its former state, a perfect medieval city. Viollet-le-Duc undertook the work and the city you see today is largely his creation.

149

There are those who will complain about Carcassonne. It may not be genuine, it has been much restored, but it looks right and it feels right. As you push your way up the crowded streets or cross the drawbridge into the keep, you feel that this is real, and if you go there in winter, when the tourists have gone, and walk round the walls, along the *lices,* the ancient lists, the sense of the past is overwhelming.

Dr Johnson once remarked that the great object of travel was to see the shores of the Mediterranean. We have come all the long miles across the Pyrénées to do just that, and we can stop here, in the *'cite'* of Carcassonne. Stop in a corner of the walls, by the Tour St. Nazaire. A piercing wind blows across the Corbières from the snowy Pyrénées and the cobbles are glazed with ice. For a while you may feel quite at home, but you are still not at home, so let the last line rest with my favourite traveller, Peter Wanderwide. Peter travelled a great deal, according to Belloc, always happy to be on the move.

> *... on his arm the stirrup-thongs,*
> *And in his gait the narrow seas,*
> *And in his mouth Burgundian songs,*
> *But in his heart the Pyrénées.*

His heart was in the right place, lucky man.

# 10 · Information

The Pyrénées is a vast area. It connects two oceans and divides two countries; it is a region seamed and grooved with rivers and valleys and it could take a lifetime to explore it properly. In this chapter I hope to provide you with all the information necessary to really get to grips with this fascinating part of France.

Some of this information has already been introduced into the text but I have gathered all this and more together here in this chapter for ease of reference. Since factual information is always subject to change it would be as well to check out travel details with the agencies concerned before you leave, but all the information here is correct at time of writing.

GETTING THERE

By road: From the north the easiest route for the Western Pyrénées is through Toulouse, via Poitiers, Angoulême or Limoges. Toulouse lies 686 km. south of Paris, and much of the Western and Central Pyrénées is just two hours drive from this agreeable city.

In the Eastern Pyrénées the focal town is Perpignan, 205 km. east of Toulouse and 908 km. south of Paris. Perpignan can be reached in a day, down the auto-routes, the A7 *Route du Soleil* to Orange, and then west along the Languedoc coast on to the B9 *La Catalane*. A two-day drive on smaller roads might be less tiring and you will see more of the country if you stop in the Dordogne or Auvergne on the way.

## FERRY CROSSINGS

Night crossings are always preferable and ensure an early start on arrival in France. Travel over on Brittany Ferries to Roscoff or St. Malo and reach Toulouse inside a day. This cuts many miles off the road south and saves both time and petrol.

Brittany Ferries also run boats from Plymouth to Santander, in Northern Spain, a 24-hour trip which will deliver you on the Southern side of the Pyrénées.

Normandy Ferries operate a service from Southampton to Le Havre which can take you South and avoid Paris.

## AIRPORTS

British airlines fly in to many airports along the line of the Pyrénées. Dan Air operate from Gatwick to Toulouse, Perpignan and Montpellier. Air France operate to Toulouse. Air Inter, the French domestic airline, flies to Perpignan, Toulouse, Montpellier and Tarbes via Paris (Orly). Brittania Airways fly into Tarbes (charter).

## RAILWAYS

The Pyrénées are well served by railways. The main route is via Toulouse on the *Sud-Express,* or the very swift *Le Capitole,* which runs from Paris to Toulouse in six hours. Within the region there is an extensive rail network connecting the main towns with local services such as the *petit train jaune* on the Roussillon linking little centres. Local train and bus services are also very adequate.

## INFORMATION CENTRES

For leaflets and information on hotels and travel apply to:-

The French Government Tourist Office,
178 Piccadilly,
London W.1.

The French Government Tourist Office — New York:-
610 Fifth Avenue,
New York N.Y.
U.S.A.

Maison des Pyrénées,
24 Rue du IV Septembre,
75002 Paris,
France.

Délégation Regionale
Midi-Pyrénées,
3 Rue de L'Esquile,
31000 Toulouse,
France.

Maison du Tourism
Palais Consulaire
66000 Perpignan,
France.

Comité Départemental du Tourism
6 Rue Eugene-Tenot,
65000 Tarbes,
France.

There are Tourist Offices (Syndicats d'Initiative) in most of the towns and larger villages.

## PHONE CALLS

Most of France is now linked by STD (Subscriber Trunk Dialling). Telephone boxes accept 5 franc, 1 franc and 50 centime coins. To obtain an overseas number you dial 19, wait for a sharp tone, then dial the national number (33 in the case of the U.K.) followed by your local area code minus the initial 0 (zero).

To dial *inter-départemental* with France, say from Toulouse to Perpignan you must dial 16 first, followed by the area code and then the number.

153

## MAPS

The Michelin (Grandes Routes) red maps No. 999 scale 1cm. = 10 km. shows main National and Departemental roads.

The Institute Geographique National (IGN) Cartes Touristique have two maps of a scale 1cm. = 2.5km. ideal for touring. You will require Nos. 113 (Pyrénées-Occidentales) and 114 (Pyrénées-Languedoc).

The Park National des Pyrénées is covered by four large scale (1:25000) topographic maps. A similar map is available for the Capcir, and a 1:50,000 map covers the Cerdagne.

Two Michelin yellow maps span the Pyrénées, scale 1:200,000 1cm. = 2km. These are No. 85 (Biarritz-Luchon) and No. 86 (Luchon-Perpignan). These give considerable detail and are very useful.

For walkers and campers the best maps are the IGN *Topographique* maps, scale 1:50,000 or 1:25,000. These are available from Stanfords Ltd., of Long Acre, London, or from shops in the Pyrénées. A certain source is from the head office of the IGN at 107 Rue La Boetie, 75008 Paris, just off the Champs-Elysées. Tel: 225-87-90. The larger bookshops in Toulouse and Perpignan stock a wide range of topographic maps and local newsagents will probably have some of the local maps.

## TOPO-GUIDES

The main topo-guides for the region are listed in the bibliography. Topo-guides are published by the Comité National des Sentiers de Grande Randonnée, 92 Rue de Clignancourt, 75883 Paris, Cedex 18. There are a number covering the Pyrénées, notably the four spanning the GR10, the Sentier des Pyrénées. The GR65 Road to Compostella crosses the Pays Basque and the GR 70 crosses Roussillon. Topo-guides can be found in most good French bookshops.

## WALKING

The Pyrénées is a great area for walking, camping and skiing. Delightful as it is, these are high exposed mountains and not to be taken lightly.

I have seen snow blocking the Tourmalet in July, needed a down jacket on the Cerdagne in August, and sunk up to my knees in new snow crossing the Canigou in early October.

The French Pyrénées seem to be mistier than on the Spanish side, so some skill with map and compass and a degree of caution would be advisable.

## MOUNTAIN HUTS AND REFUGES

The Pyrénées are full of huts and refuges, owned and often operated by the Club Alpin Français (C.A.F.) or the Touring Club de France (T.C.F.). It is advisable to join one of these clubs or an affiliated body such as the Austrian Alpine Club, if you want to use these services. Not only are the charges lower, but also members and affiliates can reserve in advance while non-members can not.

In the U.K. the T.C.F. is at the French Government Tourist Office, 178 Piccadilly, London SW1, and the Austrian Alpine Club is based at St. Albans in Hertfordshire.

## CAMPSITES

There are hundreds of campsites in the French Pyrénées, public, municipal and private. Those in or near the larger towns or villages tend to get crowded in July and August and it is as well to buy a site guide and reserve ahead.

Camping is not permitted in the *Parc National des Pyrénées* and 'wild' campers everywhere should beware of fire and remove their litter when they leave.

An increasing number of farmers have small campsites available, and *camping a la fèrme* sites are well worth investigating.

## COTTAGES AND GITES

Many visitors to the Pyrénées are now hiring a holiday cottage or gite. A list can be obtained from the *'French Farm and Village Holiday Guide'*, an annual publication available from all good bookshops.

Many villages also have what are known as *gîte d'etape,* which resemble un-manned youth hostels, offering showers, cooking

155

facilities and dormitory accommodation. The *gîte d'etape* network is expanding rapidly and is ideal for walkers and cross-country skiers.

## RESTAURANTS

The 250 mile span of the French Pyrénées offers a very wide choice of cuisine.

French hotels and restaurants are obliged to offer a tourist 'menu', or menus at prices which can vary between Fr.25 and Fr.80. Many hotels also offer a *menu gastronomique,* featuring local specialities and these are worth following. The price of a 'menu' will include service and taxes but not wine. It is usually advisable to drink either the house wine in a small jug or *pichet,* or drink the local vintage.

## HOTELS

The Pyrénées is well provided with hotels. The good ones I have discovered are listed in the text, and others may be found by consulting the 'Red' Michelin, the *Gault-Millau* guide, or the *Guide des Logis et Auberges de France.*

Two last pieces of advice might be useful. When a room is available, always inspect is before you accept it. Finally, the pillows are (usually) in the wardrobe!

# Bibliography

*South from Toulouse* by Andrew Shirley — Chatto & Windus 1960.
*The Albigensian Crusade* by Jonathan Sumption — Faber 1978.
*Guide Gault-Millau.* Annual Publication — Current issue (in French)
*Guide Michelin (Red).* Annual Publication — Current issue.
*Pyrénées — Michelin Green Guide* — Current Issue.
*Visages du Pays Basque.* Edn. Horizons de France 1946.
*Sentiers et Randonnées en Roussillon* by J. Ribas — Fayard 1978.
*Visages du Roussillon* by Yves Hoffman — Privat 1956.
*Mes Pyrénées* by Raymond Escholier — Arthaud 1959.
*Catalan France* by Basil Collier — Dent 1939.
*Guide to the Pyrénées* by C. Packe — Longmans 1880.
*Hills and the Sea* by Hilaire Belloc — Methuen 1906.
*The Pyrénées* by Hilaire Belloc — Methuen 1909.
*Gascony and the Pyrénées* by John East — Johnson 1970.
*Pyrénées East* by Arthur Battagel — West Col. 1975.
*Pyrénées West* by Arthur Battagel — West Col. 1975.
*A Concise History of France* by M.B. Davidson — Cassel 1972.

*Montaillou, Village Occitan* by E. Leroy-Ladurie — Gallimand 1976.

*Priez Pour Nous a Compostelle* — Hachette 1978.

*Haute Randonnée Pyrénéenne* by George Veron — Club Alpin Français.

*History, People and Places in Languedoc Roussillon* by Neil Lands — Spurbooks 1977.

*On to Andorra* by P. Youngman Carter — Hamish Hamilton 1963.

*Road to the Pyrénées* by Roger Higham — Dent 1971.

*Guide des Logis et Auberges de France* — Current Edition (French).

*Guide Sentier GR10* (4 vols.) Topo Guide. C N S G R (Paris).

*Guide Sentier GR77* Minervois-Corbieres. Topo Guide C N S G R (Paris).

*The Land of France* by Dutton & Holden — Batsford 1952.

*The Spanish Pyrénées* by Henry Myhill — Faber (U.K.).

*Guide Tourism et Loisirs* (Pyrénées) by Maison des Pyrénées (France).

# Index

Adour 40
Aguilar 144, 145
Ainhao 21, 38
Albères 133
Albigensian Crusade 19, 103, 104
Amélie-les-Bains 129, 131
Andorra 20, 111-114
Aneto, Pic d' (3404m) 20, 88, 90
Aragon, Kings of 19, 115, 128
Aramits 51
Arreau 76, 84, 86
Arette 61
Argelès 133
Argelès-Gazost 70, 72, 133
Ariège 19, 22, 98, 99
Arrens 69, 70
Artouste 62
Ascain 38
Aspe, *gave de* 58, 61
Aspet, *col de* 98
Aspin *col d'* 84
Aspres 128, 129, 131
Aubisque *col d'* 69
Aude 121, 142
Axat 147
Ax-le-Thermes 109, 110
Azil, Mas de 98

Bagnères de Bigorre 22, 70, 77
Balaïtous 69, 70, 72
Banyuls 22, 25, 134
Barcelona, Counts of 115
Barèges 82
Barronies 72, 77, 84, 87
Basque, pays 20
Basques 17, 26-51
Basse-Navarre 28
*Bastides* 52
Bayonne 21, 32, 46-47, 48
Béarn 25, 48, 49, 52-69

Bedous 61
Bernadette 74, 75
Bernadotte, Jean-Baptiste 66
Bertrand de Comminges 87
Betharram 68
Beziers 104
Biarritz 21, 44
Bidache 49
Bidassoa 16, 39
Bigorre 20, 68, 70-86
Bigorre, *Pic du Midi de* 82
Bouillouses 121
Bourg, Madame 116
Brèche de Roland 36, 80

Cadèac 84, 86
Cady 122
Cagots 34, 42
Cahors 24
Cambo les Bains 36
Campan 77, 84
Canet-Plage 140
Canigou, Mont (2784m) 26, 126, 128, 132
Cap Cerbère 16
Capcir 121
Carcassonne 144, 149, 150
Carlit, Pic (2921m) 22, 26, 116
*Casque du Leris* 77
Castelnou 130
Castile 39
Catalonia 17, 19, 114-149
Cathars 100, 101, 102, 103, 106, 107, 108, 109, 121
Cauterets 21, 22, 69, 70, 72, 77
Cerdagne 20, 21, 29, 111, 114-124
Ceret 131, 132
Charlemagne 35, 112
Charles the Bad 28, 57
Château de Jau 25

Ciboure 42, 43
*Club Alpin Français* 20, 62, 81
Cluniac Order 30
Collioure 24, 133, 134
Comminges 86, 87-98
Compostella 17
Compostella, Road to 22, 30, 138
Conflent 121
Couiza 147, 149
Couserans 87-98
Corbières 22, 25, 141-150
Corsavy 132
Côte Basque 32, 40

Dagobert, General 119
Départements 26

Eaux-Bonnes 69
Elne 126, 136
Envalira 113
Estagel 144
Eugenie, Empress 44
Eus 129
*Euskara* 27

*Fandango* 27
Fenouillèdes 145
Ferdinand of Aragon 28
Fitou 25, 147
Foch, Marshal 76, 93
Foix 24, 98, 99
Foix, Counts of 19, 28, 54, 73, 100
Fontfroide 147
Font Romeu 117, 118
Food 24, 32
Formiguères 121
Francis I 39, 63

Gabizos 72
Galamus, *gorges* 146
Gan 67
Gavarnie 70, 78, 80, 82
*gave* 52
Ger, Pic de 69
Gotein 38, 51
Gourette 69
Grande Randonnée (GR10) 22,
 133

Han, pic de (2074m) 108
Hasparran 49
Hautacam 77
Haute Route 22
Hendaye 40
Henry of Navarre (Henry IV) 17,
 19, 28, 63, 64
Herod Antipas 94
Hôspice de France 90, 92

Izarra 32

Jer, Pic de 77
Jesuits 32
Joffre, Marshal 93, 142
Juraçon 24, 67

Kakouetta 49

La Bastide Villefranche 52
Labourd 28, 36, 39
Labouiche 100
*Lauburu* 38
Lac Bleu 84
La Cortinada 113
La Mongie 82
Landes 48
La Pierre St Martin 26, 61
Larceveau 48
La Rhune (900m) 38
Larressore 48
Laruns 62
La Tour de France 144
Latour du Carol 115
La Trinité 130
Lavedan 72, 73, 76, 82
Lavelanet 103
Llivia 115, 116
Lombrive 109
Louis Phillipe 131
Louis XI 39
Louis XIV 15, 39, 44, 119, 138
Lourdes 73, 74, 75, 76
Loyola, Ignace 27, 32
Luchon 88, 89, 90
Luron, *neste de* 86
Luz St Saveur 77, 78

Madiran (wine) 24
*Makhila* 48
Majorque, Palais de Rois de 19,
 138
Maladeta 88
Mallorca, Kingdom of 19, 115
Maulèon 51
Mirepoix 101, 102, 103
Moncade, Tour de 54

Montaillou 108
Montfort, Simon de 96, 103, 104
Mont Louis 116, 119
Montségur 101, 104, 106, 107,
 108

Napoleon III 44
Najera 19, 28
Navarre 17, 28, 39
Navarre, Kings of 16, 17, 28
Né (Mont) (2147m) 72
Néovielle (Mont) (3091m) 71, 82,
 86
Niaux 109
Nive 30, 34, 46
Nivelle 43
Nuria 119

Odeillo 118, 119
Olette 122
Olmes, Mont d' 108
Olmes, *pays d'* 103
Oloron 58
Ordesa 71
Ornolac 109
Orthy, Pic de (2017m) 49
Ossau, Pic du Midi d' (2884m)
 61, 68, 69
Oxocelhaya 49

Pamiers 101
Park, National Park of Pyrénées
 61, 71, 78
Pas de Roland 34, 36, 37
Pau 21, 62, 63
Payolle 84
Pedro III (of Aragon) 20
*pelota* 39
Perdido, Mont (3355m) 81
Perpignan 21, 125, 136
Peyrepertuse 144
Peyresourde, *col de* 86, 88
Pla d'Adet 86
Planes 119, 120
Pont d'Espagne 77, 78
Porté 114
Port Vendres 133
Prades 119, 125
Prats de Mollo 132, 134
Puigcerda 116, 121
Puilaurens 144, 145
Puivert 103
Pyrene 110
Pyrénées 15, 20
Pyrénées, Treaty of (1659) 17,
 115, 116, 119

Quéribus 107, 144
Quérigut 121, 144
Quillan 121

Rabelais 28
Rasiguères 144
Ravel 43
Rennes-le-Château 107, 147, 148,
 149
Rigaud, Hycinthe 138
Rivesaltes 25, 142
Roland 35, 36, 80

Roncevalles 27, 30, 80
Roussillon 19, 21, 124, 125-140
Russel, Count Henri 81, 82

Saillagouse 120
Salat 98
Salses 142, 143, 144
*Sardane* 25
Sare 38
Sarrance 61
Sault, pays de 26, 108
Saunière, Berengar 147-149
Sauveterre de Béarn 52, 54
Seix 98
Serrabonne 129
Somport 30, 58, 61
Sorede 133
Soule 28, 48, 49, 51
St Anthony 49
St Beat 93
St Bertrand de Comminges 93,
 94, 96
St Étienne Baïgorry
St Francis Xavier 32
St Gaudens 96
St Genis des Fontaines 126, 130
St Jacques de Compostella 22
St Jean de Luz 24, 43, 44
St Jean Pied de Port 28, 29, 30
St Lary Soulan 86
St Laurent 132
St Laurent de la Salanque 142
St Lizier 96, 98
St Martin du Canigou 122, 126
St Michel de Cuxa 122, 126, 128
St Pé de la Moraine 86
Superbagnères 88, 89

Tarascon 109
Tarbes 76, 77
Taurinya 128
Tech 125
Têt 125
Thuir 130
Toulouse, Counts of 104
Tourmalet, col de 26, 82, 84
Toy, pays 73, 78
*transhumance* 68, 92

Urgel, Bishop of 100, 112
Urs 110
Ussat 109

Valcabrère 96
Val d'Alan 16, 87, 90, 93, 115
Vallespir 131, 132
Vénasque, Port de 90, 92, 93
Vernet les Bains 124, 128
Vicdessos 100
Viella 93
Vignemale 70, 82
Villefranche de Conflent 122
Voltaire 15

Wildlife 70
Wine 24, 67, 141, 144